To The
Domans

You are doing
great
work

Thanks for all
you do!

J Wilson

To The
Donans?
Very Best
Jim
Wishes
Wants of the
David

The **Good News** About **HARD TIMES**

James:Paul's Life-Coach and Ours

Jonathan H. Wilson

authorHOUSE

AuthorHouse™
1663 Liberty Drive
Bloomington, IN 47403
www.authorhouse.com
Phone: 1 (800) 839-8640

© *2015 Jonathan H. Wilson. All rights reserved.*

No part of this book may be reproduced, stored in a retrieval system, or transmitted by any means without the written permission of the author.

Published by AuthorHouse   08/18/2015

ISBN: 978-1-5049-2796-3 (sc)
ISBN: 978-1-5049-2795-6 (e)

Library of Congress Control Number: 2015912931

Print information available on the last page.

Any people depicted in stock imagery provided by Thinkstock are models, and such images are being used for illustrative purposes only.
Certain stock imagery © Thinkstock.

This book is printed on acid-free paper.

Because of the dynamic nature of the Internet, any web addresses or links contained in this book may have changed since publication and may no longer be valid. The views expressed in this work are solely those of the author and do not necessarily reflect the views of the publisher, and the publisher hereby disclaims any responsibility for them.

Scripture quotations marked RSV are taken from the Revised Standard Version of the Bible, copyright © 1946, 1952, 1971 by the Division of Christian Education of the National Council of the Churches of Christ in the USA. Used by permission.

Scripture quotations marked NIV are taken from the Holy Bible, New International Version®. NIV®. Copyright © 1973, 1978, 1984 by International Bible Society. Used by permission of Zondervan. All rights reserved. [Biblica]

Scripture quotations marked NRSV are taken from the New Revised Standard Version of the Bible, Copyright © 1989, by the Division of Christian Education of the National Council of the Churches of Christ in the United States of America. Used by permission. All rights reserved. Website

Scripture quotations marked KJV are from the Holy Bible, King James Version (Authorized Version). First published in 1611. Quoted from the KJV Classic Reference Bible, Copyright © 1983 by The Zondervan Corporation.

Contents

Acknowledgments ix

"Doctor Fahrenheit?" 1

"James: our Life Coach in facing problems" 15

"When You Can't Make up Your Mind" 27

"Satan, Trials, Temptation and Success" 41

"The Party invitation awaits" 51

"Dialogues of the Deaf" 63

"Bible study without application is an abomination" 75

"How to Have Successful Relationships" 87

"The Road to Success-Reality Faith" 99

"The World's Biggest Trouble Maker/Encourager" 109

"How to Relate Wisely to People" 123

"A subject that we don't like to talk about" 133

"All it takes is 57 cents" 143

"Patience in Times of Suffering" 157

"Old Camel Knees" 169

Acknowledgments

Well, after the encouragement of a lot of people, this book has finally become reality. Initially, I had only 25 copies made and gave them away to a few friends who needed material for a Bible Study. But what started getting me interested in a wider distribution, was quite unexpected. Patty and I went to my Fiftieth High School Reunion from San Bernardino High School. Before going I had tossed a couple of copies of the book in the trunk of my car. During the reunion, I got into a discussion with our former class president, Jack Wilson. His wife Marianne said she was looking for materials for her woman's Bible Study. I went out to the car and gave her a copy to review. They contacted me a couple of weeks later, and requested one for each member of the group. I said sure, and I sent them as many copies as I had, with the request that they give me some feedback as to its helpfulness.

At the end of the 15 week study I received this response:

"Our multi-denominational Bible study group was given a chance to use Dr. Jon Wilson's book on the Study of James. Many of these women have been doing Bible studies for about 30 years or more. We were very impressed with Dr. Wilson's book. Not only was it an informational study guide, it was also an anecdotal work making the information easy to apply personally. One of the women said that there were several "laugh out loud" parts, which made it a book whose successive chapters were much anticipated. Dr. Wilson's engaging ability to deliver information with gentle humor along with great insights into the book of James sets this book apart from previous study guides we have used."

Marianne's words encouraged me, along with others who read the book and also shared encouraging words.

Thus a book was born.

But a word about those Spiritual Directors in whom I am deeply indebted. I want to acknowledge many people who contributed to my understanding of the ministry, especially the Preaching ministry, either with their presence, or through their writing.

Jonathan H. Wilson

When I went to Seminary I had no idea what preparation for ministry encompassed. I guess I had a vague idea that it would prepare me for pastoring, preaching, and counseling. However as I studied Greek, Hebrew, Systemic and Biblical Theology, and diagrammed in Greek the whole book of Romans, I realized that I was not going to get the kind of practical pastoral and preaching education I thought I needed to be an effective Church Pastor. Don't get me wrong, I loved my Seminary Education, but i needed more. I was learning to parse Greek words and diagram Hebrew sentences, but I was not learning how to be a an effective pastor. I was getting the tools necessary, but I was not getting the Spiritual Direction I truly needed. I heard many great preachers and pastors in the regular Seminary Chapel services, and as I visited churches. So I began asking a lot of questions to friends about who my friends and Professors thought was a "Great" Pastor. I set out to learn ministry from Models who had done ministry that was considered by many to be successful and effective.

I began making a list of the names who came up. Soon I had a list of 50 or more names. I determined that I would study the keys to effective Ministry under every one of them. Dick Halverson, a pastor in Washington D.C. and Chaplin of the United States Senate was on the top of the list. I called him and asked if i could come back to DC and study under him. He said "Come on back you can stay at my house!" I did and I went with him everywhere for about a week. I interviewed him every night until we were both bleary eyed. On that first trip I went to visit Gordon Cosby at Church of the Savior in DC, and Lloyd Ogilvie at Bethlehem Presbyterian Church. I would call the "Great Pastors" and set an appointment with them. If they were out of the area, I would try to coordinate a trip to hear and meet with them in an interview format. I had dozens of questions. Most had limited time, so not to be denied, I ended chauffeuring many of them to speaking engagements, meetings, etc. (The longest trip was a wonderful driving interview with John Stott) If they were not available, I would try to read anything or everything that was available about them and their ministry. I got on the sermon mailing list of dozens of pastors across America. I found many Spiritual Directors, and learned from them all.

I have continued to do this to various degrees with well over 100 effective pastors and wonderful communicators in in various denominations. I have thousands of tapes, C.D. s and printed sermons.

The Good News About Hard Times

Many were Presbyterian, as that was my original orientation, but there were just as many non-Presbyterian. Almost every summer, for some 30 years we would go to the Mt Hermon Christian Conference Ground. While there I would always ask several of the Staff who the best speakers were the last year, and I would always buy their tapes or CDs and listen to them when I would drive.

My list included: Dick Halverson, Bob Munger, Doug Coe, Lloyd John Ogilvie, John Huffman, Ray Ortland, Don Moomaw, Gary Demarest, Ray Steadman, Peter Marshall, D. James Kennedy, Tim Keller, Bill Hybels, Chuck Swindoll, Rick Warren, Bob Russell, George Barna, Billy Graham, Marshall Foster, Chuck Colson, John Perkins, Roberta Hestenes, Joyce Meyer, John Maxwell, Jim Roan, Mark Brewer, Mark Patterson, Lewis Smedes, Mel White, Jim Edwards, Ben Patterson, Dale Brunner, Earl Palmer, Mark Labberton, Bert Decker, Chip Ingram, Rene Schlaepfer, D Stuart Briscoe, Craig Barnes, Charles Stanley, Adel Calhoun, Eugene Peterson, Gayle Beebe, Rich Buhler, Joel Olsteen, Tony Campolo, David Hubbard, Dave Winter, Bruce Larson, John Ortberg, Gordon Cosby, Dallas Willard, John Stott, Mike Ladra, Ken Working, John Bristol, and my covenant group, Len Sunukjian, Jay Shirley, Cal Marble, Jeff Smith, and Ken Working.

There was nothing scientific about my choices and I know there are other names that I heard preach in person or on tape, or CD, or read about, that I did not write down at the time and have failed to mention. I want to give special thanks to Rick Warren, Lloyd Ogvilie, and Rene Schlaepfer whose sermons I grew especially fond of and listened to over and over as they especially encouraged this pastors soul. Rick told a group of Pastors I was a part of more than once: that he was privileged to have a research team work for him, and he assumed that most of us did not have the resources to do that so, he invited us to use his material as long as we were honoring the Lord and giving Jesus the Glory. He told us that if we improved them to send the improved ones to him. I was grateful for an attitude like that, but I never did.

The real preparation for ministry in my life were the times listening to and studying at the feet of those Spiritual Directors, who were doing ministry, and doing it with some element of success. To those who allowed me to enrich my life and ministry by asking them questions for hours on end, I am deeply in debt.

Jonathan H. Wilson

Most of all, I want to thank my wife Patty, a great Bible teacher in her own right, who spent most every Saturday night for years editing, writing, and cutting what I had written. I would print it out, she would mark it up, and I would do a final rewrite. She has been an amazing life partner. Then to Margaret McNutt who would take my manuscript right off the pulpit, get a sermon tape or CD and retype my woeful hand writing, it providing printed copies for distribution to a mailing list. Thus recycling the material. Many others have edited various sermons over the years, and I thank each one of you for your help. I also am indebted to the Turner Foundation Board of Directors, who has allowed me to include writing as a part of my job description. It really takes a Village of Spiritual Directors.

Sincerely,

Dr. Jon Wilson
Executive Director/CEO
The Turner Foundation
300 E. Cannon Perdido
Santa Barbara, CA 93101
Jonwclergy@aol.com

A Study in James

Chapter

{1. "James wants us to become a visual aid to the unbeliever as we live out what our lips profess to believe"

James 1:22... "be doers of the word, and not hearers only"}

"Doctor Fahrenheit?"

"Five test questions checking our Maturity"

The Book of James –An Introduction

"What is Maturity?"

I can still hear the late Joan Rivers repeating during one of her famous monologues, "Oh grow up". Good advice? I tend to think so. I believe that the greatest problem that we have in this world is immaturity. People need to "grow up!" James' goal in his letter is to talk about the immature Christian. This is written, not to unbelievers, but the Book of James is written to believers. We see can that in the first two lines of Chapter One. People are acting immature, making immature decisions, acting in immature ways. Some people in life have this mysterious life-long quest to find God's will for their life. The Bible says that finding God's will is not some mysterious search for the Holy Grail with mysterious inscriptions on it from the Hebrew. The Bible, very strongly in the Book of James, points out that Christ's will for us is personal growth and maturity.

God's will for every part of creation is growth. The same is true spiritually, emotionally as well as physically. God's will for every person is that they grow to maturity. In Hebrews 6:1, "Let us go on to maturity." The word "mature" in Greek is the word "teleos", translated "mature, complete, perfect." James uses the word five times within five chapters. The Letter and the purpose of James is to bring people who are already Christians to maturity in Christ. It is a manual on maturity.

Who is James? Who wrote this letter? There are many theories about it; some say it was James the brother of John and one of the sons of Zebedee. Others say he was James, the son of Allpheus. Most competent scholars now agree that the James who wrote the letter is probably the James, the Lord Jesus' own stepbrother. As a result, we really should take James seriously as he grew up with Jesus. He had direct knowledge of the teachings; he saw the miracles. He was actually not a believer in Christ as the Messiah until the time of the Resurrection. Paul tells us that it was the Resurrection that had a powerful impact and changed James' entire life and belief about his stepbrother, Jesus. Jesus' stepbrother, James, would be perfect for the role, as men said his "knees were as callused as a camel's from long times of prayer."

James is very important in the Early Church. The time that he wrote was probably the earliest letter written about the Early Church. It took place during the time of the Book of Acts. The scribes and the Pharisees hated James, and the people loved him. He became such a significant leader in the Early Church that the great Apostle Paul came to him at least at least three times to seek advice. Today we would probable call James Paul's "life coach", for it was James that Paul went to seek counsel and advice. In the early days after the Resurrection, James became the acknowledged leader of the Early Church. In Jerusalem, even the Jews regarded James with respect and reverence, so he gained the title of "James the Just."

One of the early church historians, Eusebius, tells us that James was killed for his faith, by being pushed off the pinnacle of the temple. The pinnacle was the point in the wall around the temple that jutted out over the Kidron Valley. There is a drop of about 100 feet from the height of that wall, straight down into the valley. Years ago, I stood on that wall, on the pinnacle of the temple, and as I looked down into the valley I was reminded that this was the very place where the devil took Jesus and tempted Him to jump off the pinnacle of the temple.

Eusebius tells us that in about the year 66 AD, "James the Just," the brother of our Lord, was pushed off the pinnacle by the Jews who had become angered with him for his Christian witness and testimony. Historian Eusebius says that the fall did not kill James, and that he managed to survive the fall, stumble to his knees and pray for his murderers. By then they got so angered that they finished off the job by stoning him to death in the same fashion that Stephen was killed.

What was it about the life of his brother, Jesus' life that would dramatically change James' feelings to where he was willing to lay down his life for what he believed about Jesus? I can think of no stronger testimony than his opening words to this letter: James 1:1, "This letter is from James, a slave of God and of the Lord Jesus Christ." This is a tremendous change, because James did not believe in his brother during the times of Christ's earthly ministry to somebody who says that he is "a slave" of the Lord Jesus Christ.

The Good News About Hard Times

What caused the change? After the Resurrection Paul writes in I Corinthians 15:7, "The risen Christ appeared to James," an incident that undoubtedly led to his conversion and later as a disciple of Jesus, and a leader in the Early Church. This letter from James was written during the early part of the life of the early church. It comes out of that period reflected in the Book of Acts, and may therefore be the earliest Christian document that we have, written perhaps even before the Gospels of Mark or Matthew. You cannot read this letter without being struck by its likeness to the teachings of Jesus. In fact, if you take the Sermon on the Mount and the Letter of James and lay them side by side, you will see more than a dozen exact parallels. Therefore, it is quite evident that James listened to the Lord Jesus and heard these messages, even though perhaps he struggled with them at the time. Another thing about this letter that aligns with the methods of teachings of Jesus is that just as Jesus took illustrations directly from God's creation, so did James. You have the waves of the sea, the animal kingdom, the forests, the fish, plants, trees, and others all drawn from nature, just as the Lord himself did.

If we are to look in James' own words, I think we would see that it was not so much the words of Jesus as the works his brother did and the life he lived. Of course, the most overwhelming miracle upon James' mind was of the Resurrection. In the life of Jesus, he saw far more than mere words, far more than theology. He saw a clear demonstration of what Jesus taught. What James is saying to all who have ears to hear is "Christianity is a faith that really makes a difference, a philosophy that carries with it a life changing force." Here was a practical way of living, a realistic power to meet the problems of the day. This was a faith that worked in practice as well as in theory and to James; practicality was of utmost importance. What really concerned James was that Christians not just talk, but do good works and have Christ-like attitudes that demonstrate the genuineness of their faith.

The theme verse of James letter might well be James 1:22, "...be doers of the word, and not hearers only." In essence, he is saying that faith in Christ, if it is to be authentic, is not just words but is seen in several ways that we act:

1) by the way we deal with troubles

2) by the use of one's tongue

3) the way one handles money

4) by the non-judgmental way one treats other believers

5) by the kind of wisdom we seek

James mentions these things, not to discourage us, but rather to prune us so that we became more productive and effective witnesses to a brand of life that has the fingerprints of Jesus all over it. James wants us to help the person who says, "I would become a Christian if only I could see one."

James wants us to become a visual aid to the unbeliever as we live out what our lips profess to believe. Unlike the letters of Paul, James' letter was not focused on the particular issue of one particular church, but it was intended for all believers everywhere.

After Stephen was martyred in Acts 7 and 8, persecution intensified and believers left Jerusalem and went everywhere throughout the Roman world. These Christians did not yet have supportive believing communities, so James as the leader of the Jerusalem church wrote to them all as a concerned pastor. After he identifies himself, he writes the address. James 1:2, "It is written to Jewish Christians scattered among the nations." It is important we understand that writing this letter assumed that the people who read it already had a saving knowledge in Jesus as Lord and Redeemer. He was writing to people who were already believers, but who needed to act upon what they believed. That is called maturity—when our walk matches our talk! Throughout the Bible, one of the very purposes of the church is to help people to grow spiritually. Satan tricks us into making us think that we are mature. What is maturity? Perhaps it helps first of all to define what it is not.

1. Maturity is not age.

a. It has nothing to do with how long you have lived, or how long you've been a Christian. You can be a Christian for 50 years and not be mature.

b. Unfortunately, so many people experience severe cases of arrested spiritual development. Their spiritual development stopped when they dropped out of Sunday school in the 7th grade. They have a 7th-grade spiritual education, trying to live in an adult world with serious adult questions and it doesn't work. There is a bumper sticker that reads: "I may be getting older, but I refuse to grow up." That sticker could be on the cars of many believers.

2. Maturity is not appearance.

Some people just look mature, more spiritual than the rest of us. They appear dignified, holy, sanctified. You can wear a clergy collar, have a head full of silver hair, and still not be spiritual at all. On the other hand, I know other young-looking people who are incredibly mature spiritually, but to see them in person, you'd think they were still in high school.

3. Maturity is not achievement.

You can accomplish a lot and still be very immature. You don't have to be mature to make millions. That is attested all the time in the newspapers.

4. Maturity is not academics.

Maturity has nothing to do with how many degrees you've gotten or how much education you have. When I was a senior in high school, I thought I knew everything—and then I went to college. At the university, I found out that I didn't know as much as I thought. Then, I went to seminary, got into Greek and Hebrew and found out how little I really knew. Then I went on to get a doctorate, and now I don't know anything much at all. You can have so many degrees that they call you "Doctor Fahrenheit", but that does not make you mature.

5. Maturity is not in recognition.

Recognition is what people say about you, but that is not maturity; that is not what God thinks about you. You can have all the headlines, good or bad, and it has nothing to do with your maturity. The critical dilemma is what God thinks about us. God says that maturity is our "attitude." Attitude is what makes the difference. God says that it is your attitude that determines whether you are mature or not. God wants us to grow up and have Christ-like attitudes. How do you measure spiritually? Not by comparing ourselves with someone else. This is funny because we can always find someone less mature than ourselves to compare ourselves, but by comparing ourselves to the Word of God.

James writes in his manual on "What is Spiritual maturity?

The following five marks of maturity:

1. A mature person is positive under pressure.

James 1:2-4, "Consider it pure joy, whenever you face trials of many kinds, because you know the testing of your faith develops perseverance, and perseverance must finish its work so that you may be mature and complete not lacking anything." How do you handle trial and tests of your faith? The first test of maturity is how do you react to problems? Do problems blow you away? Do you get nervous, uptight, and negative? Do you grumble and gripe? How do you handle problems?

Christianity is a way of life; it is not really a religion. It is a life. Jesus said, "I have come that you may have life." Life means problems; and part of life is solving problems and facing them in the right attitude.

What is your attitude? When things don't go right, is your natural bent to become irritated? Are you negative or positive? Are you a supportive person or a skeptical person? Is your life filled with gratitude or grumbling? Are you affirmative or angry most of the time? James says, "Blessed is the person who perseveres under trial, because he has stood the test, they will receive the crown of life that God has promised those who love him." I know people and so do you, who go to every Bible study known to man. They are in great knowledge of the Bible, yet as cantankerous as all get out! Are you positive under pressure?

2. A mature person is sensitive to people.

James 2:8, "If you really keep the royal law found in scripture, 'Love your neighbor as yourself' you are doing right.'" A mature person doesn't just look at their own needs; they look at the needs of other people. They understand the hurts of other people. They are not only interested in what affects them, but they are very concerned with the needs of others. Immature adults, like children, tend only to see life in light of themselves. It's "me, me, my, my. I want that, I want this, I don't care about anybody else." God says that He wants us to love one another; that means being involved in the active care for another human being and that love and concern for others is a mark of maturity. In his letter, James get very specific: James 2:1-6, "Don't show favoritism, don't be a snob, don't look down on people, don't judge by appearance, don't insult people, don't exploit people." James said, I may do all kinds of things for the Lord, I may build great church buildings, I may be on TV, I may give all kinds of money to the poor, I may be a regular on the prayer chain, but if I do not have love, I am as a sounding brass and a tinkling cymbal; it just doesn't amount to much. It is interesting to me that in the Matthew 25 judgment, the one thing we will be judged for is how we treated other people—not how many Bible verses we memorized. The Pharisees were great at that. Or, not how many times we were in church, but on how we loved people.

3. A mature person has mastered his mouth.

James 3:2, "We all stumble in many ways. If anyone is never at fault in what he says, he is a perfect man, able to keep his whole body in check." When you go for a checkup, the first thing a doctor will ask you to do is to stick out your tongue. He uses your tongue to check your health. God does that, spiritually, too. In World War II there was a saying, "Loose lips sink ships!" I can say after all these years in ministry that is also true in many other areas of our lives. Loose lips destroy marriages, destroy careers, and destroy lives. One definition of gossip: "Hearing something you like about someone you don't." It is mouth-to-mouth recitation. Self-control comes from tongue control. We get ourselves in so much trouble by what we say, what we think, and what we speak. James gives us several illustrations. He says that our tongue is like a rudder, or like a bit in a horse's mouth, a spark, a snake, a spring. He says you put a little bit in a horse's mouth and that little bit can control the direction of the horse. A little rudder on a boat can control the direction of the ship. Your tongue, which by size is a very small thing, controls your life. What you say directs your life; what you say can destroy your life and all your relationships. James says that it can delight people's lives, and it can discourage people's lives. Your tongue is a powerful force for good or for evil. Have you ever heard someone say, "I just say what is on my mind"? They are actually proud of it. They say they are just being honest, just being frank, up-front, just saying what's on their mind. Not thinking that what's on their mind could be totally wrong, uncaring, hurtful, or devastating to other people—probably being judgmental without knowing all the facts. Chances are that what is on their mind should not be said. The results of those thoughtless comments are often destructive. The Bible says that kind of talk is not frankness, but thoughtless, tactless, inappropriate, hurtful, and immature. A large number of people need huge doses of tactfulness.

Ephesians 4:29, "Do not let any negative talk come out of our mouth but only that which is helpful for building up others according to their needs." Note the word, "any". Don't let any negative words come out of your mouth. Watch what you say and when you talk, it is not just not saying negative things; it is building up other people. That is a mark of maturity. A mature person manages his or her mouth. It doesn't matter how long you have been a Christian, if you can't manage your mouth you have missed the point. The third principle of our church is to keep the good report principle. That is, "I will not give or receive a bad report about another member of our leadership or congregation, but will lovingly direct such a person to go and be reconciled. I will furthermore hold them accountable to do so for their own good and for the good for the body of Christ."

James 1:26, "If anyone considers themselves religious and yet does not keep a tight rein on their tongue, they deceive themselves and their religion is worthless." Even if I've memorized a hundred verses, go to church and never miss a service, if I am a gossip my religion is worthless. If I spread rumors, it is worthless. If am always saying things that are not accurate or plant negative false impressions or exaggerate or speak negative impulsively, it is worthless. The test of maturity is to manage your mouth so that no corrupt communication, or any negative talk comes out of our mouth. Paul writes, "Speak the truth in love," that means to speak with the right attitude, the right timing, the right location, and with the right motive. The Bible is very practical. It doesn't matter how much you know about the Bible, if your attitude isn't like Christ you're missing the point.

4. A mature person is a peacemaker, not a troublemaker.

James 4:1, "What causes fights and quarrels among you? Don't they come from your desires that battle within you?" James is talking here about conflict. He says that "There are inner quarrels and fights and they come from our inner desires. You want something and you don't get it. You kill and you covet but you cannot have what you want. You quarrel and fight and you do not have because you do not ask God." Are you a peacemaker? Are you a troublemaker? Do you like to argue? Are you a contentious person? Do you get your feelings hurt? Do you get defensive easily? Do you hurt other people's feelings? Are you a peacemaker or a troublemaker? A sign of immaturity is someone who argues about everything. A contentious person! Paul wrote to the Corinthians, "You guys are a bunch of babies, you argue about everything." They argued about the Lord's Supper, gifts, leadership, everything! That is a mark if immaturity. I suggest that you memorize Proverbs 13:10, "Only by pride comes contention." Conflict is most often caused by pride. The Bible seems to say that "all conflict is ego, pride." When my wife and I have conflict, it is because I am proud and I don't want to admit I was wrong; or, she was proud and doesn't want to admit she was wrong; or we're both proud and neither of us want to admit it. Pride guarantees conflict. Another cause of conflict is seen in James 4:11-12, "Brothers, do not slander one another. Anyone who speaks against his brother or judges them speaks against the law and judges it. There is only one lawgiver and one judge, one who is able to save and destroy. But who are you to judge your neighbor?" God says that we should not judge other people. And if we do, we are asking for a fight. You are always finding fault, always stirring up strife, and always spreading rumors. Don't judge! Only God has all the facts, you don't and neither do I. Nor do we know someone else's motives. You can't tell what is in someone' heart. You don't know another person's heart, neither do I. We don't have the right to judge. Being judgmental is a serious sign of spiritual immaturity.

5. A mature person is patient and prayerful.

James 5:7, 11 "Be patient then bothers, until the Lord's coming... as you know we consider blessed those who persevere." Verse 16, "The prayer of a righteous man is powerful and effective." Note two words, "prayer" and "patience". God says that a mature person is prayerful and patient. Those are the key words of Chapter 5. Patience is used four times. Prayer is used seven times. The mark of a mature person is that they are prayerful and patient. James, in 5:7, gives the illustration of a farmer. If anyone has to have patience, it is the farmer. He does a lot of waiting. He plants a seed, waits, prays, hopes, expects—and he waits. There are no overnight crops. Just like a farmer has to wait, sometimes we have to wait. We have to wait on God in prayer. We have to wait on God for a miracle. We

Jonathan H. Wilson

have to wait on God to work in our lives. We have to wait. Patience is a mark of maturity. The only way you learn patience is by waiting.

I have learned patience on the Southern California freeway system. J Learning patience on the freeways has even messed up my spiritual life with the Lord. You see, I pray a lot in the car. I'll be cruising along and having a wonderful time of prayer with the Lord, when some jerk pulls in front of me. That is one way I have learned patience.

I do okay on the freeways now; it is just when I get into the mountains that I get into trouble. We used to go to Lake Tahoe once or twice a year and I hate those roads. It seems that every time we're on one of the back two-lane roads, we get behind some tourist who is going two miles per hour, taking photos of the mountain scenery. I remember one trip when we were behind 7 tourist busses, 16 eighteen-wheelers loaded with either cement of steel beams, 17 RV's, 8 doublewide trailer houses, and 450 cars. Now, most of those cars were being driven by people from Florida, average age of 100. These people drive slower because they have fewer goals left to accomplish in life than do I. My challenge is to get around every one of those vehicles before we reach Lake Tahoe. I figure I'll save at least 30 seconds if I do that.

Patty has always given me helpful advice in situations like that. She would like me to stop and admire the scenery, stop for drinks every few minutes, inspect all of the restrooms on the route, and maintain a spirit of happiness for the entire two weeks that it takes us to make the trip. But, the trip that taught me the most patience was the one we took about four years ago on the main southern route into South Lake Tahoe.

For the first 18 hours of Friday rush hour traffic, things went fairly well. We averaged about eight miles an hour from Sacramento on. As we got above the North Fork of the American River, where on a white water raft trip a few years earlier we had almost lost Patty—not once, but twice—as she was thrown out of the raft, it started to snow. The traffic ground to a stop. As it was an unexpected storm, the people in the orange suits who usually stop the traffic and turn you back if you do not have chains were not there. We cruised along in the bumper-to-bumper traffic. Soon, I could feel the pulling on the steering wheel, the sure sign of a flat tire. No problem, I was a patient man. I pulled off the road and got on my cell phone to call AAA. We

The Good News About Hard Times

were in a dead Zone; I could get no reception. Well, no problem, it had been a few years since I had changed a tire, but I think I did it once and knew the basics. I opened the trunk to look for the tire but the tire was no where to be seen. It was under 400 pounds of baggage and clothing in the trunk. I put everything carefully on the side of the road. It was snowing pretty heavily by now and having grown up in Southern California, I saw no reason to buy anything but gardening gloves. They came in handy for about three minutes until they were soaked through and my hands were frozen. Finally, I found a tire—only it wasn't a real tire, it was an overgrown donut and to further test my patience, there was no jack. My attempts to flag down passing motorists was a poor attempt at reconciliation for all the people I had passed on the highway between there and Sacramento. I suppose the "Lakers" sticker on the car didn't help with those Sacramento people. After about three hours of waving, I told Patty, "It might be a good idea to start praying." Then, I found out she already had been praying.

Finally, a Laker fan stopped, rolled down the window, making sure not a fleck of snow got in. He let me borrow his jack and watched from the car as I put on this donut. Originally, we had plenty of time, but now the time was starting to get precious. For you see, I had received a phone call the previous week from a "Pastor-seeking Committee" that wanted to interview me on the phone at our hotel room in Lake Tahoe. Since there was three hours difference from the East Coast, a 7 p.m. interview was 10 p.m. there. We were not sure if we were interested in the position, as we liked to look at snow, but not live it. I had been born in Buffalo, New York, and knew what it was like to live in the snow. We found out later that God had other plans for us; He wanted me here at another church, but He just had not told me that at that time.

So, the pressure was mounting. Meanwhile, the guys who stop traffic had passed us by two minutes after I fixed the flat and said goodbye to the Good Samaritan. We ran into a roadblock where my worst suspicions were realized. We had to turn back to Sacramento unless we had chains. We were going to meet our youngest son Jonny and his snowboarding buddies at Tahoe and we had this phone interview, so that was not a good option. The only other option was that we could pull off to the side and pay some guy our entire life savings to buy two chains, only one of which would fit. We bought two, paid several hotel night's stay for them, and a mile down the road the one

Jonathan H. Wilson

on the donut fell off and I pulled off to the side of the road, totally unable to put it on in any secure way. Well, we made it to the hotel on one chain a few hours later, but it was close to midnight East Coast time and to say the least, we did not find a warm reception as we were all tired and exhausted. During that trip I learned some important lessons.

I learned, again, why my Mom moved us from the East Coast and why I didn't want to live in the snow, but more importantly, I learned the difference between "No" and "Not yet." I think I used to believe that a "Not yet" means "No." Sometimes God will say to us "Not yet." He doesn't mean "No." He doesn't mean He is not going to answer your prayer. He is saying, "I have something better for you—not yet—I want you to wait, I want you to develop, to grow, to mature.

Following are five questions to test our maturity.

I re-learned many of them that night.

1. How do you handle problems? Do you get uptight, negative, grumble, gripe, and complain? Or, are you positive under pressure?

2. Are you sensitive to other people? Are you concerned about other people's needs, desires, cares, hurts, or do you only see yourself?

3. Can you manage your mouth? Have you learned when to muzzle it and not speak? When you have a juicy tidbit of gossip and it's tempting because knowledge is power, do you pass it on, or do you pray about it? Or, do you pass on gossip in the form of a prayer request? You can damage people by innuendo.

4. Are you a troublemaker or a peacemaker? Do you have a tendency to stir things up? Do you have a hair trigger where someone can set you off quickly? Do you carry a grudge? Do you find yourself nursing bitterness? Or, are you a peacemaker? Have you learned as Paul wrote in Ephesians, "Let no corrupt communication, no corrupt talk come out of our mouth, but only that which builds up for the edification of others according to their needs."

5. How long can you wait for an answer to prayer without giving up? Maybe God has every intention of giving it to you, but he is waiting to teach you maturity.

So, how do you rate? James makes all of us squirm a bit. He flashes on the screen of our consciences the inconsistencies and sins of all believers. But remember it is done, not to discourage us, but to prune us to be more effective. James wants us to help that person who says, "I would become a Christian, if only I could see one." This is not an easy message, but it is one we all need. Thank God for James, the brother of Jesus!

{"There are some lessons in life we only learn through pain. Pain is God's megaphone to get our attention."

Psalms 117:71 "I used to wander off until you punished me; now I closely follow all You say. The punishment you gave me was the best thing that ever happened to me, for it taught me to pay attention to Your laws"}

"James: our Life Coach in facing problems"

Book of James – 1:2-6

When our son, Jonny, played varsity basketball in High School, we always went to as many games as possible. I thought about this passage in the context of his basketball season. Jonny's team was at one point 12-5. They could have a far better record, but the coach chose to play the pre-season against much larger schools. In the preseason, they played teams such as last year's State Champion in a higher division (more students in the school), and the current year's favored championship team. As a result of playing stronger teams, i believed that they were better when it came to the regular season.

This is also true with football teams. When a football coach wants to build a good team, he does not send it out on the field with soft pillows. He puts it to work against rough opponents, and he puts it through exercises that are hard and strenuous. That is what James is talking to us who are members of his team. He is a life coach.

James is, perhaps, the most tough and direct book in the Bible. However, James was no armchair quarterback. He was speaking from the perspective of one who had been through difficult times. He was the brother of Jesus, who he had watched Jesus go through unwarranted persecution, false trials; and, he had watched him die at the hands of murderers. James, himself, had been through a lot of difficult times.

James is telling us how to lasso the bucking, uncontrollable trials of life and ride them to wisdom and triumphant spirituality. He instructs all those who will listen how to go through suffering without becoming hardened, and learning wisdom necessary to plow victoriously through life's many trials. James is a "how to" manual for living a Christian life—from one who has seen the hardest trials of life and learned how to rise above them.

God does the same thing with us to give us the strengths of steadfastness and patience in our character. He marches with us against tough opponents, against temptation, against public opinion, against discouragement and depression. In quite a different way, it is the same principle that I heard from a grower who spoke at Rotary this week. It is interesting to me that good fruit are produced only under the stroke of severity. Apples do not grow where there is no frost. There are no clouds on the Sahara desert, but neither are there flowers. Tears are as important in the Holy Spirit's cultivation of the "fruit of the spirit" in our lives, as rain is important to grow flowers and fruit.

Normally, writers warm up to and then gradually get to their message, with perhaps a few prelims, opening remark, and then the message. However, James drops the bomb in Verse 2, "Consider it pure joy, my brother, whenever you face trial of many kinds..." What if someone sent you a letter like that—you got problems? Be happy in many, many trials! Friend, you just don't understand.

The key is because you know, "Consider it all joy, my brothers, whenever you face trials of many kinds because you know that the testing of your faith produces perseverance." Your level of understanding determines your attitude. Rejoicing is not just positive thinking, but is based on some facts of life. Here are some remarkable facts that will help you with the problems you are in right now.

I. Facts of Life... "because you know..."

a. Problems are inevitable – It doesn't say, "if" it says, "whenever you face trials". You can count on it. If you don't have problems, check your pulse. Problems are a fact of life. They are a required course, whether in dating, marriage, sports, school, or life in general. You don't get out of them by saying you don't want to have problems. Nobody is immune. Of course, problems are really inevitable if done by stupid people, which reminds me of a story that appeared on newswires this week: Dateline...Little Rock, 1-04-03, An Arkansas man was arrested after robbing a bank. He smashed a glass door, looked directly at a security camera, and set off an alarm. The money had been stashed away because the bank was closed, so he stole a clock radio and a handful of candy. As he left, he ate candy and tossed wrappers all the way to his home at a nearby trailer park. Police simply followed the candy wrappers to his home and arrested him. He was arraigned on robbery charges, with bail at $25,000. The candy that he stole was called "Dum-Dums". ☺ Of course, problems are really inevitable if you are stupid and break basic laws.

In Scott Peck's classic book, The Road Less Traveled, the first sentence is "Life is difficult..." That is the message of the book. It is true that it is inevitable that you will have problems in life.

The Good News About Hard Times

b. Problems are unpredictable. "...whenever you face trials." The word "face" is Greek "peripipto," and means to fall into unexpectedly. It is the same word used in the story of the Good Samaritan to describe the man who fell among the thieves. It was unexpected. Trials are never planned. We fall into them. We seldom can anticipate the problems we are going to experience in life. That is probably good because if we could anticipate them we would probably run the other way and would get no benefit from them. We don't have to plan a flat tire, an accident, or a health crisis. They are unplanned and unpredictable and come when least expected. Essentially, that is what makes a problem a problem. If it was expected and you were prepared, it wouldn't be a problem.

There is a story of a guy on a New York subway for the very first time. He was overcome by motion sickness and was standing in line next to the door. The subway stopped, the door opened and he lost his lunch on the guy standing first in line to get on the subway; the door closed, and the train took off leaving the guy standing there asking "Why me?" ☺ Problems are unpredictable.

c. Problems are inconvenient. "...trials of many kinds." Problems come in all shapes and sizes. So we don't get bored, they come in a large variety. For example, I had to go for new prescription glasses this week where I was supposed to be "In and out in an hour!" Baloney! After an hour-long check up there were hundreds of decisions about size and kind of frame, and other issues. This store advertised an "In and Out in an Hour" offer. However, that is only if you get a quick and certain kind of prescription that fits the frames that are already on the shelf. Problems come in all different sizes and shapes.

d. Problems are purposeful. "Realize that they come...to produce in you." They have a purpose. Pain can be productive; suffering can accomplish something in our lives. I have given you these two words before, but I've been told I have to repeat something every 28 days before people begin to remember it. The two words are: "Suffering produces." What does suffering produce?

1. Problems purify my faith. "...you know that the testing of your faith..." James uses the word "testing" as in testing gold and silver, i.e., you heat them up until the impurities called the "dross" was burned off. Job understood this, saying, "He has tested me through the refining fire and I have come out as pure gold." The first thing that trials do is

to test our faith. They purify us. Someone has said, "Christians are a lot like tea bags; you don't know what is in them until they are dropped in hot water." Then you know. Your faith is developed as things don't go as planned. Your faith is developed when you don't feel like doing what is right, but you do it anyway. It purifies your faith. Christians are supposed to be like steel, when they are tested they come out stronger. Many of you are in the midst of testing right now. You are enrolled in a course called "Character Development."

2. Problems fortify our patience... "...the testing...develops perseverance" Here, James is talking about staying power—not passive patience, but staying power, endurance, the ability to "keep on keeping on," the ability to hang in there. The Greek is literally, "the ability to stay under pressure." We don't like pressure, and we do everything we can to avoid it. We run from it, take drugs, drink alcohol, and go to Disneyland, anything to get away from pressure.

The story is that the Pope got tired of the pressure of always being the Pope and pampered all the time. He just wanted to be a regular guy who could do regular things.

One day, after getting all Pope John Paul's luggage loaded into the limo, the driver notices that the Pope is still standing on the curb. "Excuse me, Your Holiness," says the driver, "would you please take your seat so we can leave?"

"Well, to tell the truth," says the Pope, "They never let me drive at the Vatican, and I'd really like to drive today." "I'm sorry but I cannot let you do that. I'd lose my job! And, what if something should happen?" protests the driver, wishing he'd never gone to work that morning. "There might be something extra in it for you," says the Pope.

"Reluctantly, the driver gets in the back as the Pope climbs in behind the wheel. The driver quickly regrets his decision when, after exiting the airport the Supreme Pontiff floors it, accelerating the limo to 105 mph. "Please slow down, Your Holiness!!!" pleads the worried driver, but the Pope keeps the pedal to the metal until they hear sirens. "Oh, my Lord, I'm gonna lose my license," moans the driver.

The Pope pulls over and rolls down the window as the patrolman approaches, but the policeman takes one look at him, goes back to his motorcycle, and gets on the radio. "I need to talk to the Chief," he

The Good News About Hard Times

says to the dispatcher. The Chief gets on the radio and the policeman tells him that he had stopped a limo going a hundred and five miles an hour." "So bust him," said the Chief. "I don't think we want to do that; he's really important," said the policeman. "All the more reason!" says the Chief. "No, I mean really important," said the policeman. "What'd ya got there, the Mayor?" "Bigger." "Governor?" Bigger! "Well, said the Chief, "Who is it?" The policeman said, "I think it is God!" "What makes you think it is God?" "He's got the Pope driving for him!" ☺

Even if we were the Pope, we can't escape being human, having problems. If we did, it would just reduce our ability to grow from them. God teaches us patience in traffic jams, in long lines at Costco, in the waiting periods of life. We live in a society that worships comfort, convenience, and fast service. Everybody wants it now, if not yesterday. Endurance today is a rare quality. I believe it was Vince Lombardi who once said, "When the going gets tough, the tough get going." An old cliché, but true.

II. Problems strengthen my character. They help me to mature, to grow, to become more like Jesus, James writes, "so that you may be mature and complete, not lacking anything." You have seen the bumper sticker, "When life hands you a lemon, make lemonade!" It is easier to smile at that than practice it, but the philosophy is sound and in fact, biblical. Throughout the Bible are people who turned defeat into victory, trials into triumph. Instead of being victims they became victors. James tells us that we can have this same experience today. That is God's long-range goal for us. His ultimate purpose is our maturity. God wants us to grow up, to mature. In the Christian life, character is the bottom line. So very many Christians have absolutely no idea of God's agenda in their life. They don't know what is happening so they are overwhelmed by their problems.

God's number one goal in life is to make you like Jesus Christ. Listen carefully, God is far more interested in developing your character than He is in developing your comfort level. If God is going to make us like Jesus, then He has to allow us to go though the things Jesus went through. There were times when Jesus was lonely, tired, tempted, depressed, and discouraged. The Bible says there are two ways that God makes us like Jesus.

a. James 1:22-25, "The word makes us like Jesus." It builds our character; it matures us. But how many of us really read it? This is the number one way God speaks. In 2 Timothy 3:16, "The whole Bible was given to us by inspiration from God and is useful to teach us what is true and make us realize what is wrong in our lives. It is God's way of making us well prepared at every point." Notice it says that God's way of talking to us first is through His Bible. The Bible is not just a good collection of wonderful thoughts and ideas of men, just a nice inspired collection. "Inspiration" literally means in Greek, "God breathed." That means that the Bible is absolutely reliable. There is no other book in the world that is reliable like this book. It can be counted on. It will guide you. It will correct you. It will comfort you. It will help you. However, if you never get in it and don't read God's letters to you, how can God talk to you? This is why it is so important to have a time where you sit down and read it, better yet in one of your Bible study groups. It doesn't matter the amount of time. You see, you talk to God in prayer and you let God talk to you through His word. If you're not doing that on a daily basis, you're missing the number one way God wants to talk to you. Someone says, "God never talks to me." The question back is "Are you studying the Bible?" This is how He wants to speak to you. If you're not reading the Bible, your phone is off the hook. He is getting a busy signal and He can't get through to you.

If I told you that tomorrow the President of the United States wanted to meet with you at 4 p.m. in the courthouse in Los Angeles, I don't care what you think of the President, you'd get up and you'd go. When somebody that important wants to meet with you, you go. Even more important, God wants to meet with you tomorrow and you don't even have to go to LA. You can do it in your own backyard, or sitting at your coffee table with a cup of coffee, or in a big La-Z-Boy chair with your pj's on. He is waiting. The Creator of the universe wants to have a conversation with you all the time, on a regular basis. You need to get into God's Word because this is the number one way that God speaks to us. If the only time you're in it is every other week or so, you're going to miss a whole lot and starve spiritually and your life will be confusing. Now, I understand the Bible can be an intimidating book. In the first place, how many other books do you know that are bound in leather? I've met some non-believers that don't even want to touch it! How many other books do you know that has a number before each sentence? That's kind of strange. And, if you use an old translation you have the "thee's" and "thou's" and lots of words you don't understand and some strange names and strange places and foreign words and customs that don't make sense. The Bible can be intimidating, but on the other hand it is as good, in fact better than gold. The Bible is a practical manual for life and James, in my estimation, the most practical letter in it. It is the owners' manual for life, written by the One who designed it.

A few years ago, we bought a new car. In the glove compartment was an owner's manual. That is the designer's original intent for the car. If I read that owner's manual and follow what it says the car is going to last a whole lot longer. It teaches me how to keep my car going! That is what the Bible does. Why many people are under stress is because they don't know what is in the Bible and they're not following what it says to do. So, they are stressed out. The Bible is the owner's manual for life. When in doubt, consult the manual. God speaks through His Word. God demands even more the second way.

b. The circumstances of life. Here is where James hits it right on the head. So many Christians say, "Things were going great until I became a Christian, then all the problems came. Maybe God doesn't love me. Maybe I'm not a Christian. Maybe I'm not really saved; maybe I missed the boat." Nope! You are right where God wants you. You're in a character course. He is making you like Jesus. Romans 8:28, "We know that all things work together for good (not all things are good) if we love God and are called according to His purpose." He wants us to be like Jesus. He wants us to have the Fruit of the Spirit. How does God teach us the fruit of the spirit—love, joy, peace, patience, kindness, etc? By putting us in exactly the opposite situation. If God wants to teach you love, He puts you around unloving people. If He wants to teach you joy, He puts you in difficult circumstances so you will learn joy in the midst of the situations. If He want to teach you peace, God put you in chaos. Think about it. The phone rings, the computer catches a virus, you lose everything you've been working on. The dog starts barking like crazy at the man-eating squirrels in the backyard. That is where you learn peace. It is easy to learn peace while sitting on a beach in Maui. Anyone can do that. We learn patience through waiting. Paul says in Ephesians, "We are God's workmanship." God wants to make a "masterpiece" out of you. He wants us to become perfect, complete, not lacking anything. That is a picture of Christ. That is what He wants us to be like.

III. Problems fortify our patience.

a. Rejoice. "Consider it pure joy whenever you face trials..." Don't misunderstand this. He is not saying to fake it, to put on a plastic smile, to pretend and be a Pollyanna. God never asks you to deny reality. He is not telling us to get psyched up. Nor, is He talking about masochism. "Good, I get to suffer. I just love to suffer. I feel so spiritual when I suffer." He doesn't want us to have a martyr complex. We don't rejoice for the problem, but in the problem. We don't thank God for the problem. Why would we thank God for evil? But, we can thank God in the problem. I Thessalonians 5:18, "In everything give thanks for it is the will of God concerning you in Christ Jesus." If you want to know God's will for your life, it is simple "In everything give thanks." Nor does it say to give thanks to God for giving you leukemia, or the accident, or the war, or that you lost your Mother. No way! What kind of God would that be? It says, "In everything give thanks." Why? It means that we can thank God because we know that God can take even the bad in our lives and turn it around and bring good out of it. I don't care where your problems come from. You may have caused them yourself. Satan may have caused them. They may be a problem that society has brought upon you. It doesn't really matter the source of your problem. God can use that problem for your growth and for His glory. What makes the difference is your attitude. It says, 'Consider it pure joy..." The word "considers" means a deliberate look at it. It means to evaluate, to make up your mind once and for all. While I'm living in the present, I look forward to the benefit of it. Consideration is a choice. He is not saying "Grin and bear it." Listen carefully, rather that we are to count it joy, and behave in such a way that the negative experiences become transformed into matters for rejoicing. Although we cannot control the circumstances that happen to us in life, we can control how we will respond to them.

Victor Frankl, the psychologist who spent time in a Nazi concentration camp in Germany writes, "They stripped me naked. They took everything—my wedding ring, watch. I stood there naked and all of a sudden, at that moment, I realized that although they can take everything away from me—my wife, my possessions, my family—the one thing they couldn't take away from me was my freedom to choose how I was going to respond." You choose to rejoice, it is an issue of the will, of choice, not of feeling. It is better to say you act your way into feeling, rather than feeling your way into acting. Psalm 34:1, "I will bless the Lord at all times. His praise shall continually be in my mouth." Even when I don't feel like it, even when things are not going right, we bless and praise the Lord. You see, problems do not automatically produce blessings. For some people, problems destroy them; others are made better. You'll either be bitter or better. The difference between bitter and better is "I"—I make the difference with my attitude. Problems break some people; problems make some people brittle. It is how you choose to respond. Choose to rejoice.

Brian Hise had more than his share of bad luck one July day a few years ago. His apartment in Provo, Utah became flooded from a broken pipe in the upstairs apartment. The manager told him to go out and rent a water vacuum. That is when he discovered he had a flat tire. He changed it and went inside to call a friend. From the electric shock he received from the phone, he inadvertently ripped the phone from the wall. Before he could leave the apartment the second time a neighbor had to kick the door down because water damage had swollen it so tight. While all this was going on, someone stole his car. But, it was almost out of gas, so he found the car a few blocks away but he had to push it to a gas station where he filled up the tank. That evening he attended a military ceremony at his university. He injured himself severely when he somehow sat on his bayonet, which had been tossed on the front seat of his car. Doctors were able to stitch up the wound, but no one was able to resuscitate four of his canneries that were crushed to death from falling plaster. After Hise slipped on the wet carpet and badly injured his tailbone, he said he wondered if "God wanted me dead, but kept missing." ☺ Now, that is a good attitude. How you choose to respond to difficult situations is your choice.

God speaks through pain. Are you acquainted with this idea? I have said it before; we don't change when we see the light. We change when we feel the heat. None of us really like to change and so we fear what it might do to us. We fear change and we don't change until the pain of not changing becomes greater than the fear of change. Once the pain is greater than the fear, we change. God is so interested in speaking to you and so interested in having a personal relationship with you, of loving you and your loving Him and being able to talk about everything that He will even resort to this in order to get your attention. Proverbs 20:30, "Sometimes it takes a painful experience to make us change our ways." Every one of you knows this one by experience. Now, not all pain is God speaking to you. Not every little hurt, ache, and pain that you have is God. But, some of it is. God often has to use pain in order to get our attention.

An all-star basketball player had back trouble and had a bunch of disks that went out. His pastor asked him in the hospital, "Why do you think this happened?" He said, "God had to lay me flat on my back to get me to look up to Him." Has God ever had to do that to you? There are some lessons we only learn through pain. David in the Psalms writes, "I used to wander off until you punished me; now I closely follow all you say. The punishment you gave me was the best thing that could have happened to me, for it taught me to pay attention to your laws." Pain gets our attention. It is God's hearing aid. As I recall, it was C. S. Lewis who said, "God whispers to us in our pleasures, but He shouts to us in our pain." Pain is God's megaphone. When you're hurting God is saying, "Hey! There's somebody here who wants to help! You can depend on me. I'll help you through that tough time if you'll just let me." Pain is God's way, often, of getting your attention.

b. Request. Of all times to pray, it is when you have problems. What do you pray about? "If any of you lacks wisdom, he should ask God who gives generously to all without finding fault, and it will be given to him." When you are in the middle of problems, you pray for wisdom. Why should we pray for wisdom? So you don't waste the opportunity to grow and mature. If you don't learn this there will be one more lap around the desert. God will give you another opportunity to learn the lessons He wants you to learn from this problem. We become overwhelmed when we don't understand what God is doing, so pray for wisdom. Wisdom is looking at things from God's perspective. Pray for wisdom to understand the problem. There is no situation in life that we cannot learn from, if you have the right attitude. Don't ask why, asking that question will drive you crazy. Ask "What?" What can I learn from this problem? What, Lord, do you want me to learn from this situation? What do you want to teach me in this problem? What characteristics do you want me to develop?

c. Relax. Trust God to know what is best for your life. Co-operate with His purpose so you won't short-circuit the process. That is what is called "faith!" "But, when he asks, he must believe and not doubt..." Relax, and let God work. Friends, it breaks my heart when I think about the heartache and pain so many of you are going through right now. Some of you are going to be in "God's Hall of Fame" because of your faith. You have maintained a sweet spirit in the face of incredible pressure. Things that people did to you, that people have said about you, situations with which you have been living. It's not always easy to have a joyful heart in the midst of difficult situations. Even when you have a joyful attitude, it is still difficult. That is why you need to

The Good News About Hard Times

pray for two things: (1) Wisdom to understand the trial; and, (2) Faith to endure the trial. You need them both.

This reminds me of the story of the little Catholic girl, who before Christmas got down on her knees, put a statue of Mary in front of her and said, "Dear Lord, I would like a bicycle and a new doll for Christmas." The next night she got down and prayed, "Dear Lord, I would like a bicycle and a new doll for Christmas." On Christmas, she was doubting whether she would get the bicycle and doll so she took the statue of Mary, Mother of Jesus, and put it in the drawer and then prayed, "Dear Jesus, if you ever want to see your mother again..." ☺

James says we need wisdom to know what is going on and faith to hang in there and never give up. You're never a failure until you quit. Some of you are going through tremendous problems right now. It's pretty hard. God cares. He cares very much about you. God sees everything you are going through. He's got your number. In fact, He knows the number of hairs on your head, according to Scripture. He knows exactly where you are. He hasn't lost your number. He cares. God has the power to do something about the problems. He could change it in a snap. He is a miracle-working God. Why doesn't He? Because, He's got a greater purpose. The greater purpose is what God wants to do in your life. God is far more interested in building your character than in making you comfortable. Once you've learned that lesson, He may be free to remove that situation. However, there are some things in life we're never going to be free from, this side of Heaven. There are thorns in the flesh. We will deal with them and carry them throughout life. But, nothing comes into your life without the Heavenly Father's permission. There is a wonderful promise in Scripture in Verse 12, "Blessed is the person who preserves under trial. When they have stood the test they will receive the crown of life that God has promised to those who love him."

God says there will be a reward. I don't think when we go to heaven the rewards will go only to the pastors, evangelists, and the Billy Grahams. I think many of the rewards will go to the people who quietly persevere through the difficult situations and develop the character of Jesus Christ in their life. He says that there will be a crown of life. Cast your cares on Him. James tells us how to lasso the bucking, uncontrollable trials of life and ride them to wisdom and triumphant victory. Satan wants to use problems to defeat you; God wants to use your problems to develop you. Which will it be?

{"There are some lessons in life we only learn through pain. Pain is God's megaphone to get our attention."

Psalms 117:71 "I used to wander off until you punished me; now I closely follow all You say. The punishment you gave me was the best thing that ever happened to me, for it taught me to pay attention to Your laws"}

"When You Can't Make up Your Mind"

Book of James-

1:5-11

Every single day of the year we make dozens of decisions. Some of those decisions we are happy with, others we come to regret. Frank Borham once said, "In some ways, we make decisions and then our decisions make us."

One day a young businessman went to his mentor in business and asked, "What is the secret of business success?" The man said, "Wise decisions." "How can I make wise decisions?" Answer, "Experience!" "How do I get experience?" "Dumb decisions." ☺

Every day we make dozens of decisions, some wise, some not so wise. Some of you have a very difficult time making decisions; some of you will be faced with very difficult decisions this week, maybe even tomorrow. Life is full of decisions and choices.

James tells us how to make decisions, how to make up our minds. He gives us the problem; then he gives us the prescription; and then he gives us the promise from God.

I. The problem: indecision based on feelings and emotions.

Chapter 1, Verse 8, "A double minded man is unstable in all his ways." In Greek, "double-minded" means two-souled, pulled apart, divided loyalties, divided priorities." You have to make a decision, and you're not really sure what you want to do. Perhaps you've heard the story by Dr. Seuss:

Getting on a horse and going off in two different directions does not work. When you've got to make a decision, double-mindedness is devastating, paralyzing, and debilitating. In the Bible, the word is used in several places to describe a confused person; as drunk who would stagger across the street.

James is saying that if you can't make up your mind, it produce's an unstable lifestyle. Indecision makes you unstable in three ways:

Jonathan H. Wilson

(a) Unstable Emotions—It is a strain on you emotionally when you are indecisive. You worry, can't sleep, can't eat right, and you become confused and anxious. You wonder if you did the right thing. It creates emotional instability. A guy goes to a counselor who asks, "Are you indecisive?" He guy said, "Yes and no." The counselor asks, "What do you mean by that?" The guy said, "I used to be, but now I'm not so sure." ☺ William James said, The most miserable man in the world is the person who is habitually indecisive.

(b) Unstable relationships—Lack of commitment to decisions destroys marriages. When you can't decide, "Do I want in or do I want out?" "I can't get on with it; I can't get out of it." "What am I going to do?" As parents, it creates problems, too, because when we say one thing to our children and then do something else, it creates instability giving double messages. When we are unstable in our jobs, always switching back and forth between careers it, again, creates emotional instability. I think that, many times, it takes more energy deciding than it does to do it. Once you decide to do it, it's a snap—the key is deciding!

(c) Unstable Spiritual life—Verse 7, "...that man will not think that he'll receive anything from the Lord." Instability blocks your prayer life. If you keep changing your mind as to your request from God, how does God know what you really want to receive? How will you know when you have what you have been praying for? Have you ever said, 'Why doesn't God answer my prayers? Maybe you've never really decided that you will honor God's wisdom if He gives it. If you haven't made that decision to do what he says, then He is not going to reveal it. He senses when we are ready to do it. Double-mindedness can lead to a double life, a spiritual schizophrenia such as in Dr. Jekyll and Mr. Hyde. From Pilgrim's Progress, do you remember "Mr. Facing Both Ways?" That is when you want to do God's will and yours at the same time. When you know what is right, but you do wrong anyway. Verse 8, "A double-minded man is unstable in all his ways." The problem is indecision. What is the solution?

II. The World's prescription for indecision: "It's all relative."

Change your values, morals, and behavior, according to what is popular or being sold or pushed by society. Can you imagine President Bush changing his mind based on the daily public opinion polls about whether or not to go to war? How unstable would that be?

The Good News About Hard Times

I think that Sadam is counting on public popular opinion to pressure the President to change his mind; but I don't think Bush has bought into public opinion as the wisdom at the base of his thinking and integrity.

In 1966 an American Professor named Joseph Fletcher wrote a book entitled, Situational Ethics, which has proved to be one of the most influential books of the last 100 years. Fletcher's basic principle was that there "is nothing which is universally right or wrong, good or bad." For the situationalist, there is one thing and one thing only that is absolutely always and universally good, and that one thing is love. The ultimate guide for decision making is what is the "loving thing." But what is the "loving thing?" It depends on who is asking and who is responding.

Let's look at a historical example: On the wilderness trail, Daniel Boone's trail west through the Cumberland Gap to Kentucky, many families lost their lives to Indians. A Scottish woman had a baby that she was breast-feeding. The baby was ill and crying, and the crying was betraying her and her other three children and the whole wagon train. The party clearly could not remain hidden if the baby continued to cry. The baby did; the baby crying compromised their position and they were all massacred. How would doing the "loving thing" have helped her make her decision?

On another occasion there was a black woman with a crying baby in her arms. The baby's crying, was also threatening to betray the whole party. Difficult as it was, she strangled the baby with her own hands to stop its crying, and the whole party escaped.

Which action was love? The action of the mother, who kept her baby and brought death to it, to herself, and all the others; or, the woman who killed her baby and saved the lives of the caravan? Both were. They both did what they thought was the "loving thing," but their actions were opposite. We are not helped in those kinds of decisions with love as our only guideline. It doesn't always work. The truth is that Fletcher was trying, quite successfully I might add, to get us away from making decisions according to a standard and to make them based on our feelings of emotion. How would love help us make a decision? It depends on whom you talk to and how they justify it. The Taliban would probably tell you it is their love for God that helps make their decisions to murder innocent people. Reality is this, listen carefully, most people make decisions based on feelings, not facts. They make decisions based on feelings and then justify those decisions with facts. You may resist this statement. You may want to shout, "No! No! No! I am a rational, cognitive human being? I make calm, considered, well-thought-out rational decisions! I do not decide on emotion!"

Listen again, contrary to our academic training, most people make decisions based on feelings and then justify those feelings with facts. Here is the proof: Think back to a major decision you made, big purchase such as a car or house, your choice of college, your first job, or the person you married. These are major life-affecting decisions. Each of us likes to think that we made such decisions in a fairly, if not completely, rational way. But let me ask you this: When you were making that big decision, did you take out a yellow legal pad, write "Pro" and "Con" at the top, listing all the reasons for deciding yes or no? Not likely! And, if you actually did that, did you make your choice purely on the basis of the weight of those answers? What, then, were the primary, scale-tipping reasons for your decision? I am not saying you didn't do research or give the decision a lot of thought. I am saying that most of our major decisions are overwhelmingly influenced at the emotional level, the "feeling" level, rather than seeking the wisdom of God. We, in effect, decide at that level and then use our intellect to justify our decisions. The fact that we decide on an emotion level is a natural fact, neither good nor bad. Sometimes, buying on emotion or feelings get us into trouble. Then, sometimes we get lucky. An emotional decision isn't necessarily the wrong decision. There is no shame in admitting we are emotional creatures and that emotion has a powerful driving influence on everything we do, think, and choices we make.

I drive a convertible; and, yes it has over 100,000 miles on it but I didn't buy it based on Consumer's Report magazine for its long record of driving. It was a good purchase. I bought it based on subjective feelings, and then justified it by getting a really good price. I bet you do that all the time. In fact, it is foolish not to admit it. The truth is, if you want to make good decisions you have to be aware of the (1) emotional issues, (2) rational issues, and (3) seek wisdom from the Lord.

So you say, "Let your conscience by your guide" to make wise decisions. Is the conscience really a good guide? Do the terrorists

The Good News About Hard Times

who bombed and killed thousands in New York, Washington and Pennsylvania really feel bad about what they did? The clear instruction of Scripture, according to Romans 2:15 is that our conscience can produce conflicting thought that either accuse or excuse our behavior.

In our time, there is so much confusion between morals and ethics that are often used interchangeably. They have become virtually synonymous in popular usage, yet historically they have distinctly different meanings.

Ethics comes from the Greek word, "ethos" derived from the root word meaning "stall", a stable dwelling for horses. It conveys the idea of stability and perseverance. An ethic does not change.

Morality, on the other hand, comes from a Greek word "mores" which describes an ever-changing behavior pattern of a changing society. Ethics tells us what to do based on God's unchanging values and God's eternal wisdom; morals tell us what society is doing. The text, which I can't get away from quickly, says in Verse 5, "If you need wisdom...ask God." The facts are knowledge. Don't act on impulsive feelings. "If you need wisdom...ask God." True wisdom does not come from the minds of popular opinion polls or the morals of society. "Morals" describes what people actually are doing, so that is ever changing. When morality is identified with ethics, then people do what they feel like doing, based on the particular group with which they hang out. Even if conscience is based on God's revealed word, we will have wisdom that will be stable. If conscience is based upon what everyone else is doing, it will be ever changing according to which way the wind is blowing. For example, if the majority in our society decides that living together is the norm, then being married is considered deviant behavior in that society and yet it was God's plan and design. That is why Paul, in Romans, says the conscience is an unstable guide for behavior. A conscience, to be a wise guideline for making wise decisions, must be based on God's wisdom, on God's eternal ethics, and on God's unchanging stable values.

III. Questionable prescriptions for decision-making

These include things that are sometimes taught, but are not, in my opinion, consistent with God's will.

(a) God's will is not fixed. When we seek wisdom, God does not give us a map, a blueprint that if we lose it we are lost. If that were true and if we feel that we had blown it, we would become fatalistic and we would wonder, "Why bother now, I've blown it!"

(b) Putting out a fleece. (Judges 6:37-40) In the Old Testament, Judges 6:37-540, we have the story of Gideon and the fleece. From that story some have gleaned a popular phase in making a decision, "I'll put out a fleece," but when we do that we are in effect setting the rules, "Lord, if you want me to do that, then you must do this." "Lord, do you want me to go to the mission field in Hawaii, or in the Bahamas?" We set up our own boundaries. We set up our own timelines, not necessarily God's. Jesus had told the apostles to wait for the power of the Holy Spirit, but the apostles got impatient. They were going to choose Judas' replacement by casting lots or putting out the fleece. Instead of waiting on God they, in effect, flipped a coin between two men they thought qualified. Neither was God's choice. They chose Matthias who was never heard from again. God's choice was the Apostle Paul.

(c) A feeling. (Verse 6) As I have said before there are those who nevertheless want God to stir their emotions, to put a quiver in their liver, to feel an ocean of emotion. The problem is that feelings are unreliable. Feelings can come from fatigue, from hormones, from a negative experience, or just watching television. Many times in the past have we made decisions based on feelings and then later realized they were wrong. Feelings lie.

(d) A magic formula. Making a good decision is not done by a magic formula. Formulas appeal to us, and that is why we buy so many of the "ten easy step" books, such as Cooking for Dummies, An Idiot's Guide to Building a Nuclear Reactor; Embalming made Easy. ☺ We want step-by-step solutions for the most difficult, complex decisions. We think it works that way because television has conditioned us that any problem can be solved in 30 minutes, minus 6 commercials. We want everything easy. We like instant messages on our computers. Who has the time, for goodness sake, to write a letter and wait for snail mail to bring an answer? We want instant messages, instant answers, easy decisions. Unfortunately, formulas often contradict one another. And, as for the 57 easy steps to making wise decisions, what if you leave out No. 39? Does the domino theory apply if we

The Good News About Hard Times

make a mistake? Most, if not all, of the Great Saints in the Bible have made serious mistakes and it doesn't say that God gave up on them.

(e) Easily found. (Job 33:14) "God does speak sometimes one way, sometimes another, even though people do not understand it."

IV. God's prescription: God's will relates to Godly wisdom

(Verse 5) "If any of you lacks wisdom..." James seems to throw in a little sarcasm here. He knows we all worship knowledge, not wisdom. We have degrees for knowledge not medals for wisdom. Wisdom is different than knowledge. Wisdom is putting knowledge into action. Wisdom is seeking life from God's perspective.

(a) Admit your need of wisdom in the midst of confusing moral values. Proverbs 11:2, "When pride comes, then comes disgrace, but with humility comes wisdom." Pride blocks wisdom. You can't learn anything if you know it all, already. Admission of the lack of wisdom is the beginning of wisdom. "I don't have it all together." "I don't have all the answers." "I don't know, God, show me what I'm supposed to do."

(b) Remember the stages.

(1) I tell Him. Ask God for wisdom; He promises to give it. Most of the time we want God to baptize our plans, "Lord, I am going to do this, please bless my plans."

(2) God responds. As we begin to do what we feel what God wants us to do, God begins to speak to our hearts. Recently, I talked with a person who admitted, right off the bat, that she was doing something that she clearly knew was wrong. She knew it was wrong, but continued to do it. I hardly said anything. A month later I talked with her again and she said she had done the right thing and for the first time in a long time had finally found peace. A peace that she said came when she finally did what she knew God wanted her to do. I see so many people that do not have peace because what they are doing is clearly outside God's will.

(c) I beg to do it anyway. (Proverbs 16:1-2) That's when we say to God, but "God you want me happy, don't you? Just let me do this; I have my heart set on it." So we struggle with God.

Jonathan H. Wilson

(d) I give up. We, at this point, humble ourselves and listen to His voice and make a decision based on His word or His voice. We say "uncle." It is obvious that what I am doing is not working, so I'll do it your way, God."

(e) God reveals. (1: 6) "When you ask him, be sure that you really expect an answer." God doesn't usually reveal His will so that we may choose whether or not to accept it. That would make us God. When we are ready, not to debate it, but to do it, then He begins to reveal His will.

C. Ask God in faith for wisdom and listen. Verses 5-6. Proverbs 2:6, "If you need wisdom, if you want to know what God wants you to do, ask him and he will gladly tell you." Look again at how the Lord gives wisdom. "...ask God who gives..." In the Greek, this is in the continuous tense. We keep on asking for wisdom, He keeps on giving. The Bible says we have not because we ask not. I bet I ask God for wisdom 20 or 30 times daily. Someone calls on the phone; I pray and seek wisdom as I pick up the phone or as I respond to E-mail. God is always willing and able to give us wisdom. Proverbs 2:6, "It is the Lord who gives wisdom, from him comes knowledge and understanding."

D. How is God's wisdom found in His word?

a. Through Bible study. Psalm 119:105, "God's word is a lamp unto my feet and a light to my path." In Israel in New Testament times they didn't have high beams on their cars nor did they have Ever Ready batteries. How did they walk at night? They had tiny little lamps that would not spill out the oil. They would light them and tie them to the front of their feet. As they walked, the light would reveal just the next step. God's light in His word does not reveal all His will, nor give us wisdom once and for all, for the next 20 years of our lives. We have to continuously seek it. He wants to give you wisdom one step, one day at a time. Now, we are talking about the "dip and do" method of receiving God's wisdom out of His word. One guy felt that he would just flop open God's word without any help and just do what it says. He opened up his Bible looking for direction. He shut his eyes, stuck his finger on a text to discern God's will and he read the verse, "...and Judas went out and hung himself." Thinking there must be something more, he again shut the Bible and again opened it and stuck his finger in to see what God wanted him to do. The text said, "Go thou and do likewise." Figuring that the third time would be the charm, he opened it again, placed his finger on a verse and it said, "Whatever thou doest, do it quickly." ☺ If you want to have wisdom, you need to get it from His word and hopefully in some kind of informed systematic method. He doesn t give us searchlights for the distant future. He gives direction one day at a time. It s not so much a dip and do method as it is pray and wait.

b. Receive God's wisdom through teachers and preachers who interpret. Have you ever been in a group and felt that God was speaking directly to you? The fact is that God, at that moment, was speaking directly to you. Teachers and preachers of God's word are called by God to interpret His word. That is why we should never miss church; not because we will feel guilty, but because we may miss some word of wisdom from the Bible that may change our lives.

c. Through impressions. Sometimes God speaks through ideas, hunches, and insights. In the Bible, it is the still, small voice of God. Always these must be consistent with God's clear word in the Bible. Decisions made in quiet times of prayer and reflection on God's word will most often be the right decisions.

d. Through circumstances. Another way is through circumstances that create pain in our lives. If we can't learn through difficulties that create pain in our lives, we're bound to get off track in our lives.

e. God wisdom is found in relationships. If we truly want wisdom we have to seek wisdom from a relationship with God. I want to read from a book I have been reading called The Leadership Genius of George W. Bush. It has only been out a few days. This is not a Christian book; it was on the new release table at Barnes and Noble. Of course, during the campaign, we were all made aware of his somewhat wild college life. Now we see a strong leader now, but we don't hear much about the personal values, which guide his decisions. This is not a Christian book, by the way, but was written by a secular author. From page eight, I quote:

The list of Bush's personal values is extensive: accountability, cooperation, freedom, fun, and others. At the top of the list, though, are three in particular. From our research, these core values assume primary importance for him. They are really what matters to him

Jonathan H. Wilson

deep down. Bush's three personal core values are (1) Family; (2) Faith; and (3) Integrity.

A story from Karen Hughes about her son provides one example of Bush's genuine concern about families. Hughes' 12-year-old son was playing in a championship Little League game just when his mother, Karen, was in the midst of an important campaign swing. When Bush became aware of this conflict, he took her aside and told her to get on the next plane and go see that game. Reflecting on this incident, Hughes said, "My boss was running for President, but he enabled me to make every game except one." The message is loud and clear; family is more important than a job. The same is true of Bush's Christian faith. He reads the Bible, openly accepts Jesus as his personal savior, and attends the White House Morning Prayer meetings. When pressed by reporters to defend his view, Bush responds, 'It's me. It's what I am all about. It is how I live my life. It's just part of me."

Relationships, family, and with the Lord...integrity about those priorities for a busy President are what he seems to be all about. No wonder he has incredible wisdom and strength to make wise, unwavering decisions in the midst of one of the most difficult political times in human history. Double-minded, he is not! A Dr. Suess character, he is not. Dr. Facing-Both-Ways, he is not. Let me personalize this: As a teenager I was lost with no clue what I was supposed to do with my life. I struggled in school with no motivation. The only thing I was good at was math and science. I could accumulate knowledge if I was interested in the subject, but I had zero wisdom. I had been to church, a very formal one, where I found it to be stiff and boring—a waste of time. In the middle of my junior year in high school, we moved to a new town where my Step-dad could be closer to his work. I went to a new high school, which was much larger, and I was lost. I immediately went out for the tennis team in order to have something to do after school. A new friend on the tennis team invited me to a Christian Youth Group. I told him, "No thanks," as I had no wheels. I thought that would finish it, but he kept after me. He said, "That's all right, I'll pick you up." Through the persistence of that friend, I came to the youth group and eventually into a life-changing relationship with the Lord. It was in that relationship with the Lord that eventually I found the wisdom to get through life. However, it did not come quickly. I still found myself facing the end of high school with no plans whatsoever. As a

The Good News About Hard Times

math-science major, I had thought I might become an engineer, so I applied at an Institute of Technology. I was accepted, but as I began to pray about it and ask God's wisdom, I thought about it and decided I wasn't so sure that was what I wanted to do. I had no peace. Since I had changed my mind about being an engineer, at the last minute, I went to a local junior college. Someone asked me to help out with the Youth Group and that had such an impact on my life. I enjoyed that, but still had no idea what I wanted to do with my life. I began to pray desperately for wisdom. I had to enroll in general education courses, so I took speech for the first time. I was so scared giving my first three-minute speech that I couldn't remember anything. I panicked and ran out of the room with the students laughing, never wanting to go back. I was unmotivated, never studied and was close to flunking out of college. Then, I faced a reality. During the Vietnam War, if you were not in school, you could expect to be introduced to Uncle Sam on an intimate basis. So, it was study and bring up the grades or go to Vietnam and duck bullets and bayonets in swampy foxholes. I started to take classes seriously. I went back to speech class and met with the speech teacher, Dr. Stallings. I'll never forget her because she threw out that big "F" and gave me another chance; I would get double credit on my next speech. I had been humbled and the Lord says that is the beginning of wisdom. Proverbs 11:2, "...with humility comes wisdom..." I began to do well in the speech class. A few months later I was asked to speak at the Christian Youth Group; and I was scared to death. Even though it was very hard, I enjoyed it and seemed to get a good response. Then, I was asked by the Youth leader to be a counselor to groups of kids from the Youth Group at Forest Home Christian Conference Center in Redlands. I really enjoyed working as a youth counselor, helping them. As I counseled kids who were only a year or two younger than I, I began to find out what it meant to pray for wisdom from God. I began to feel that maybe the ministry would be an option, though I didn't tell anyone. I began secretly praying for wisdom and asking God for His clear direction. While I was working with high school kids at Forest Home, they had the Annual College Briefing Conference. I went to the meetings, even though I wasn't enrolled in the camp, and the speakers really challenged us to consider ministry. It was out on a huge rock overlooking the valley at Forest Home that I began to earnestly pray, in fact to beg God for wisdom for my future. However, for months there was no clear-cut message from God. After junior college I transferred to Cal State, Fullerton, and began to take courses that would prepare me for any number of careers, but entirely different than the engineer that I had thought I would become. I also had considered law and teaching. I took all the speech, sociology, and psychology classes I could get into my schedule and continued to pray for wisdom about my future. I also got a job as a Resident Advisor in the dormitory. I'll never forget a phone call that I made that seemed so insignificant at the time, but turned out to be major. On the night before Easter, I called the "Dorm Mom." I called to tell her that I'd be in about noon the next day. I didn't have a great faith, but strong enough to know that church was where I wanted to be on Easter Sunday morning. I was surprised that she was upset. She said, that I could sleep in until noon, as there would be no returning students to check in until the afternoon, but that she wanted me there. Finally she said, "You can come in and keep your job, or go to church and I will expect your resignation." Without hesitation, I said, "I won't be in until after church, about noon, and if that means my resignation, then you have it." The next morning I went to church at St. Andrews Presbyterian Church in Newport Beach. After the service, I met Reverend Jim Moore, one of the Assistant Pastors. As we talked, he seemed interested in me and then he asked for my phone number. He said that he wanted to talk to me about something. He called me the next day, we met, and he offered me a job working with kids in the church for exactly the same amount of compensation that I was receiving as a Resident Advisor, starting the day I had to quit. At that time, it had been over two years since I had begun praying for wisdom and clear directions and guidance as to whether I should go to law school and into politics, graduate school and teaching, or seminary and the ministry. As I got involved in church ministry, I realized how much I loved it. As I looked back I began to realize that on that Saturday night before Easter Sunday, God had answered my two-year prayer. He had made it clear what my priorities were and what He wanted me to do. He gave me the decision for which I had been looking.

Now that God had led me to make a decision, the rest fell into place. Prior to that I had been unable to make a decision. I had been unable to make up my mind about anything, but God in His grace and mercy had showed me that when I live by His principles, such as the importance of growing spiritually in His word and seeking His wisdom, He would in His time answer our prayers. That is probably the most I've ever shared about my experience as a Christian, and

The Good News About Hard Times

I share it not because it is dramatic, there is no lightning bolt out of the blue. Frankly, I have not seen God work that way. It was a simple, but constant, prayer that I prayed for a long time. A simple experience that led to a simple decision, through which God radically changed my life. I encourage you to pray and seek God's wisdom. He promises that he will give us wisdom in any decision that we need to make if we pray and ask Him.

"Sometimes God has to test us and allow us to be 'Broken' before we realize that it is God we are here to please, and not some ever changing human standard"

Phil 4:8 "think on these things, things that are good, positive, honest"

"Satan, Trials, Temptation and Success"

Series: Book of James - No. 4

James 1:11-18

Luke 4:1-13

Temptation of man is probably the oldest problem in all of God's Word. It goes right back, of course, and originates with Adam, himself. In the Bible, there is some confusion, in fact in our Bible Study, over trials and temptations. The confusion comes from the fact that the Greek word is used for both, so it is the context in which you have to figure it out. The Greek word is "peirasmos". When it is used as trials, trials come from God to help us grow. Temptation, on the other hand, comes from Satan to cause us to sin. We need to clearly understand the difference between trials and temptations.

In our text, it says "Blessed is the man that endures temptation, for when he is tried he shall receive the crown of life, which the Lord has promised those that love Him." In other words, if we go through life and we endure and deal with temptation, there is a reward. The reward is that we will be blessed, which essentially means that we will be happy. Happiness comes, Biblically, when our life is under control, so that that there is no devastatingly bad habit that has control of you. When you know how to say "No" to temptation, it produces happiness in your life. It also means, as James says, that there is a "crown of life" waiting for us. That "crown of life" is in itself, the sense of abundant life. In other words, when we understand temptation, when we overcome it, when we are able to say "No" to the temptations of life, then we really begin to live life the way God designed it to be lived. The question is how we handle temptation. James gives us five principles to understand:

1) You undoubtedly will be tempted. James says in Verse 13, "When you are tempted..." Not if you are tempted... Remember that he was talking to Christians, so obviously, all of us can be tempted. Just like trials, temptation is inevitable. Have you ever heard someone say, "No, I've never been tempted"? That's what I say when you cross a crocodile with an abalone. You get a crock of baloney. ☺ Everybody is tempted you, I, everybody! We never get too old for temptation; we

never get too spiritual for temptation. The fact of life is that the reality is that we are all tempted. There is a misconception, here. Some people feel that once you have been, in effect born again, that you have it all together and that you won't be tempted. That is not true. James was writing to Christians, to believers, telling them to watch out for temptation. 1 Corinthians 10:13, "No temptation has seized you except that which is common to man." We are in the same boat. We all experience similar temptations, same problems, we can't hide from them, and we shouldn't be shocked by them. Maybe you are in the midst of one of those kinds of temptations right now. The ideas that temptations to man, to all of us, should be liberating knowing that other people have the same struggles and problems. It is not a sin to be tempted. It is a sin, however, to give in to temptation. Hebrews 4:15, "Jesus was tempted in all ways as we are, yet he sinned not." He was perfect; but he was tempted. Yet, he did not sin. Another thing is that we should not be intimidated by temptation. You think, "How can I have such and such a thought?" That is because Satan works in our minds. It is not your fault when you have those kinds of temptation. You are human and you are going to be tempted, so expect it.

2) Don't blame God and others for your bad choices. Verse 13, "When tempted, no one should say 'God is tempting me,' for God cannot be tempted by evil, nor does he tempt anyone." We love to blame people. We love to blame even God for our problems. Will Rogers, a great theologian, said, "You could summarize American history with two great movements: the passing of the buffalo, and the passing of the buck." Our society has become one of irresponsibility. Blame society, blame government, blame environment, blame heredity, blame parents, blame spouse, blame politicians, blame Satan, and even blame God. There is a book out entitled, A Nation of Victims, about how we have all become victims in America. Some say, "It must be God's will or it wouldn't happen." One guy said that God had told him to leave his wife and marry someone else. That, my friend, is blaming God for our own choices. Don't make bad choices and then blame God. God does not tempt us, and God never contradicts His own word. He is not going to tell you one thing, and then have written in the Bible something else. If the Bible says something and you say something different, then you are wrong. That is the way it works, if indeed, you believe that the Bible is God's Word. Don't play the blame game.

3) Take responsibility for it. Verse 14-15, "Temptation is of your own evil thoughts and wishes. These evil thoughts lead to evil actions." The reality is that most of our problems are brought on by our own mistakes. If we ever want to get rid of bad habits, we have to be realistic that we are going to be tempted; and, we have to take responsibility and stop blaming someone else.

4) Be prepared for temptation. "Each one is tempted by his own evil desires...don't be deceived." When it comes, and know that temptation will come, the Bible says the old Boy Scout slogan, "Be prepared." Peter, you will remember, said, "Be on your guard." Jesus said, "Watch and pray that you enter not into temptation." Paul said, "Put on the whole armor of God." We are to anticipate temptation, not to be surprised by it. We need to recognize that God is strategizing for your life, right now, and you need to be prepared. Temptation does not warn us in advance. It always catches us by surprise. You must be ready and on your guard. And, we are most vulnerable after a great success. We think we are doing well. The Bible says, "Let him who thinks he stands, take heed lest he fall." I think of a fellow by the name of Bobby Leach who went over Niagara Falls in a barrel and came out unharmed. A couple of days later, he slipped on an orange peel and broke his leg. It is the little things that kill us. James is saying, be ready at all times; don't be deceived by a measure of success.

a. Desires. "Each one is tempted, when by his own evil desires." Most desires are okay. You couldn't live without certain desires. A desire to eat, drink, sleep, the sexual desire, to accomplish. God gives us our desires. They are good gifts, but any desire to control them becomes destructive. The addiction to any of these things, the obsession becomes the problem. It's the fulfillment of a legitimate desire in the wrong way, at the wrong time, and to an extreme. So how do we prepare for temptation? How do we get ready? First, we understand how Satan operates. II Corinthians 2:11, "In order that Satan might not outwit us we are not to be unaware of his schemes." The Lord wants us to know how Satan operates. Satan is very consistent. He has been operating now for more than 2000 years. He pulled out his best temptations against Jesus in the passage in Luke 4. In Verse 2, "Jesus was on a fast for 40 days in the wilderness. He told Jesus to make food out of stones." That is the temptation at the point of physical need, is it not? Jesus was fasting. He was starving. Satan comes along and says, "Just turn this stone into bread; then

Jonathan H. Wilson

you can eat." What other physical addictions do we have? Food—overeating, anorexia, bulimia. And, what about drink? It is one of the basic physical needs that we have that can be abused. Rest is a need we have that becomes procrastination and laziness. Satan is the one who rejoices when people become lazy, or procrastinate, or have to rest up on Sunday mornings because of a late Saturday night. Exercise is another basic necessity of life. However, addiction to exercise can cause people to spend hours standing in front of mirrors, worshiping their bodies and who wins? Satan wins. Anything in excess can be a temptation of Satan. Sex is a good thing, but when it becomes a passionate obsession, Satan wins.

b) Deception. "He is dragged and enticed." James used a few words from the sports world. "Dragged away" is a hunter's term that means literally, "snared in a trap." Enticed is a fisherman's term, which literally means, "lured by bait." The secret of great fishing is in the bait. My next door neighbor invited me over to watch the Super Bowl. At halftime, he showed me his dad's fishing tackle box that had hundreds of different kinds of bait. There was different bait for every kind of fish in every kind of water. So it is with Satan. He uses different bait for different people. In the Luke passage, Satan claims to have the ability to give all power to whomever he wants. It is true. Paul said it in II Corinthians 4:4, he calls Satan the god of this world, "...but he exaggerates his authority." I John 4:4, "He who is in you is greater than he who is in the world." Jesus says "The ruler of this world has no authority over me." The point being, the temptation is that Satan is the master of exaggeration. A lie can easily be thrown out, but an exaggeration can be worse than a lie. People hear a partial truth and manipulate the result to favor their own feelings. Many exaggerations have destroyed many people as well as many churches.

c. Disobedience. "Then after the desire has conceived, it gives birth to sin." One of Satan's greatest temptations is the temptation to power. Luke 4:6-7, "If you will worship me, it shall be yours. Satan offered Jesus power over 'all the kingdoms of the world.'" Satan offered Jesus power over all the kingdoms of the world. Power attracts powerfully. Why? Power has a way of enhancing a person's self-worth. I've heard Chuck Colson, many times, talk about Watergate. Nixon, he said, had it all won, all wrapped up. However, when a person is put into position of power you find that the power never satisfies. Satan knows that, "Every taste of power is like a shark's first bloody bite, just creating a desire for more and more and more." But desire goes beyond power if someone can't get it, and someone else has it, they try to bring him or her down, sometimes with lies and exaggerations. Proverbs 6:16 says, "There are six things the Lord hates, no seven things he detests: Haughty eyes, a lying tongue, hands that kill the innocent, a heart that plots evil, feet that race to do wrong, a false witness who pours out lies, and a person who sows discord among brothers." What begins in your mind, results in action. You begin to think about some sin, you know it, but soon you begin to become obsessed. In that Proverb, God says that he hates a false witness, a person who sows discord among the brethren. In that temptation, negative thoughts become bigger and bigger until it results in action and God hates it. It is sheer disobedience and the end result is death.

d. Death. The text in James says, "Sin, when it is full grown, gives birth to death." That is the tragic consequence of giving in to temptation. What is death? The exact opposite of living! If you overcome temptation, you get the crown of life. However, the wages of sin is death—spiritual separation from God. You see, we can choose the way we want to live. God gives us the freedom of choice. While we can choose the way we want to live, we can't choose the consequences of our choices. The rebellious child does not choose his own punishment or discipline.

5) Refocus and replace.

Verse 17, "Every good and perfect gift from above, coming down from the father of the heavenly lights who does not change like shifting shadows." Notice that James, in Verse 17, suddenly switches gears here. He has been talking about temptation, and then all of a sudden he turns and begins talking about the goodness of God. It almost seems as if he forgets what he is talking about, but not so. He is simply refocusing from man's sin to God's goodness. He is redirecting our attention on something else.

6) Pray, share, and avoid. Proverbs 14:16, "A wise man turns away from evil, but a fool is arrogant and careless." The Bible tells us to avoid all tempting situations. If chocolate is bad for you, don't even walk near the chocolate candy store. What is the payoff of living a godly life and resisting temptation? James said, "Blessed is the person who endures temptation for when he is tried he shall receive

the crown which is life...which the Lord has promised to those who love him."

As I close I want to share with you an area of my own personal temptation. Early in my ministry, I kept hearing the phrase, "God has great things in store for you; you are going to be a great preacher with a huge church." That was of course music to the ears of a young man looking to the ministry, but it was also a curse. As a result of expectations, I began to see success in the ministry as having a big, growing, multi-staffed church. I devoted myself wholeheartedly to my preparation for ministry. I studied the great churches of America and my expectations for myself ran very high. As I studied large, growing churches, I began to equate [here is the temptation] bigness and growing church with success. Unfortunately, 90% of Presbyterian churches in America were declining.

I was encouraged to help the denomination begin to turn around and begin growing again. After all, George Barna, the expert in church growth, had studied the church where I was a pastor and used it as a model for churches that had been on a decline and wanted to turn around. The research came out in his book, The Turnaround Church. The church where I was a pastor had been shrinking for 20 years, but during the 15 years that I was there we saw major growth. I designed a new sanctuary; I had 40 weddings a year; I had a weekly radio show, I did radio, and TV debates. Also, I wrote a newspaper column for the old LA Herald Examiner.

I was a success and as a result of that, another bigger and so-called better church that had also bought into the church growth success syndrome came after me, and I bought it hook, line, and sinker. I was really impressed with myself. I figured the bigger the challenge, the better. Then, I could write the book that everyone was encouraging me to write. I interviewed and when I accepted.

Now, I became the "church growth expert," speaking at several Presbyteries, speaking as the Presbyterian Church growth expert. I was asked to speak at the Annual American Church growth convention. That led to being asked to serve on the National Evangelism Committee of our denomination.

After two years, I was then asked to serve, representing "Evangelism and Church Growth" on the highest ruling body of our denomination, the General Assembly Counsel. I flew back and forth to headquarters in Louisville and all around the country, doing conferences and speaking as church growth expert.

I was also elected as the Presbytery representative for my Presbytery to the Annual General Assembly meeting, and then asked if I would give the nomination speech for one of the three candidates for Moderator of our denomination. The candidate went from being an unknown to 40% of the vote on the first ballot. I had arrived! Several people told me that I should have run for Moderator.

Meanwhile, I went back to my new church. Everyone told me that it was just a matter of time until this new church was rewriting the book on how to turn around a large power church. We are most vulnerable after a great success. I found out that bigger wasn't at all better.

It didn't happen. I gave it my all, I was now off all national committees, but I kept writing a local newspaper column and was on the radio, working 24/7. I found out that Satan knew my weaknesses. All the church growth experts said the same thing. Things would have to change if the church was to turn around, there had to be a change in attitude towards growth. The "no-growth, no change" opposition became formidable. I thought everybody wanted to grow and would be willing to do what was necessary to grow. I was not prepared. I was also wrong. The "no change" advocates used money, withholding at certain times from the budget and then designating their giving to control and to stop change. They also kept themselves in positions of power. I couldn't believe it. The power brokers carefully organized an attack on both Patty and myself. We couldn't believe it. The bright future of that church was melting around me. The old power brokers waged a full-on attack, and I blamed God.

I began to question everything. James 1, Verse 13 was true to me at that time. I wasn't sure that God even cared. God is tempting, therefore, God is not good. Why? Why would God call me to a turn around church growth and then put me in a church that said they wanted to grow, but to do it without any change or without ruffling anyone's feathers. I found it hard to imagine people could be against reaching out and bringing new people into the Kingdom. I was leading people to Christ almost weekly and getting them into small groups before they left my office.

Jonathan H. Wilson

Both, Patty and I were naïve. I went into the deepest, darkest depression of my life. Satan was winning. I was questioning God, my faith, my calling. I checked out law school, broadcasting, writing books, teaching, and real estate. I wanted to do anything but ministry.

I share this because I want to underscore my own wretched experience because I know that many of you have felt that way at times. Satan had hooked me with the "success syndrome." The temptation of Satan to try to please everyone, to make everyone in the church happy while reaching out to God for them. I was trying to please everyone—the intellectuals wanted theological dissertations, while the mentally challenged wanted simple basic messages. There were those who wanted verse-by-verse or it was not of God; others wanted the great themes; others wanted practical sermons—always comparing you with the strengths of another pastor while skipping over their weaknesses.

We sometimes think evil of God when He calls us to a different direction and 13 people have 13 ideas about which way is the right way. Sometimes God has to test us to allow us to be broken before we realize that it is God that we are here to please and not some ever-changing human standard. Sometimes He tests us by allowing Satan to tempt us at our point of vulnerability; but the blessing is that He has promised that he will not test us beyond our breaking point. My temptation seemed so good. I wanted the church to grow, but I realized that I had bought into the world's view of success—numbers, attendance, offering plate, and number on roll. God, in His mercy, knew He wanted me free from the "success syndrome." Why? Because that is the next step in overcoming temptation. Be realistic, be responsible, be ready, be refocused, and replace negative, sinful thoughts with productive thoughts. Philippians 4:8, "Think on these things, things that are good, positive, honest."

Pray, share, and avoid. The most powerful source of strength for breaking bad habits is to seek God's strength through prayer. James says that being born again gives us a new capacity to resist temptation. You and I don't have enough power in our own willpower. We need supernatural power. That is what it means to be reborn. Pray and ask Christ to come in and clean up your life, and to give you the power to overcome your temptations.

The Good News About Hard Times

Also, we need to share as we can with prayerful non-gossiping believers. We need a support group of praying people who will uphold us in prayer. James 5:16, "Admit your sins to each other, that you may be healed." Get into a small group Bible study to find healing. We were not meant to fight the battle alone. We are all in the same boat; temptations are common to man. Revealing your feelings to the right person is the beginning of healing when we have been broken. When we have gone through a divorce, or someone we love is taken from us, as we fail from human standards, we need not to be naïve, but to be aware of the dominating force of evil in human experience. God is good, He can be trusted to pick up the pieces of this "old cracked pot," glue us back together and use us again. James says to us in Verse 16, "Don't be deceived, my dear brothers." This is a command from James, Jesus' half-brother, who watched Jesus' be broken on the cross and his blood shed.

Remember that Satan is alive and well today. Be on guard. He knows your point of vulnerability. Out of the storms of life come the flowers of growth. After the night, the sun comes up; after death comes the resurrection to new life.

Verse 17, "Only good comes from God." Yes, God allows us to go through pain, suffering, and testing, but James reminds us that He is a good God who does not tempt us, but He does test us. Why? He tests us to strengthen us, to be blessed.

Verse 12, "God blesses the people who patiently endure testing. Afterward they will receive the crown of life that God has promised those who endure testing."

Ben Franklin said, "the problem is not that man has been made in the image of God, the problem is that we have made God in the image of man"

James 1:18 "we are the crown of all His creatures"

"The Party invitation awaits"

Series: Book of James – chapter 5

James 1:16-18

James, the half-brother of Jesus, writes in this section of Scripture, "Don't be misled about the relationship between good and evil and the Father's love."

1) How can we be misled about the Father's love? Verse 16, "Don't be mislead my dear brothers and sisters." What is it that God wants us to feel about Him and how Satan uses the things of this world to distract us from feeling good about ourselves, from feeling about ourselves the way that God wants us to feel? Perhaps it is because the world teaches us in so many different ways that we are accepted based upon our performance.

a. Family Performance. Montague, a professor of sociology at Rutgers University said, "The American home is the most dehumanizing institution in the world because it teaches performance for acceptance." It goes something like this: "Clean up your room and I'll love you," "Be home on time and I'll love you." Perhaps subtle and not directly said, but there is the implication that if you perform acceptably in the family then you will be accepted.

b. Educational Achievement. As it goes on in our family, it also goes on in our education system. In fact, our whole educational system is based upon the premise that you are accepted based upon your performance. That is what grades are all about. If you get good grades, you will be better accepted. If you get grades high enough to get into the college of your choice, you will be esteemed among your fellow men. The whole premise and basis of our educational system has to do with performance in order to be accepted. It is also the whole basis of our athletic system.

c. Athletic Recognition. Who is it that gets the coach's recognition, the scholarships to college, the admiration of the fans? It is the athlete that performs most acceptably. I don't know if you have been watching this high school "phenom" that is on the front page of all the newspapers, including USA Today. He is being attacked in many ways, but he is a high school "phenom" and will be the number one draft in the NBA. He is esteemed; he is valued because he is a good basketball player. He performs! And, that is what the world teaches us over and over again. In our social system it teaches us the same thing.

d. Social Image. Who is it that gets invited to be a member of the social club, the local Rotary or Kiwanis? The one with the best image, the best family background, job, position, status, career gets the offers.

e. Economic Status. Performance is the basis of our whole economic system. The advertisers tell us over and over again that if you smell a certain way, you will be accepted. If you don't smell a certain way, you won't be accepted. Or, if you had a certain sparkle when you part your lips, you will be accepted by using their toothpaste. The whole basis of our society's economic system is based upon "You need what we have to sell in order to be accepted and if you don't, you won't." The American culture places extreme value on outer beauty and appearance. We value youth, beauty, athletic ability, intelligence, education, wealth, and fame. But, what happens when you lose it all? What happens when superman becomes wheelchair man? What happens when a super model gains some weight or gets super old? What happens when the superstar ends up in jail or addicted to drugs? What happens when you have a super career or job and you lose it? What then? Has your worth changed, or just your feelings of worth? Where do you get your feelings of esteem and self-worth when everything on which you have based your value has vanished? That kind of self-esteem that says, "I'm worth something because I am doing well and others look up to me for my performance," is a dark hole from which many people never escape. We are anxious when we don't know if we will be accepted. Our whole self-image is dependent on what others think of us. That is why they had such a hard time understanding Jesus. He came into a world of performers and didn't force anyone to perform. Jesus threw out all the merit badge systems, and the religious people high up the ladder of pretense didn't understand it or want to understand. They were sitting around having a great time at the dinner party when a prostitute came in and circled around the table. Everybody froze and when she got to Jesus she washed His feet and dried them with her hair.

The Good News About Hard Times

After everybody had recovered from the shock, acquisitions were leveled at Jesus. You remember that He responded by telling a little story. When the story ended, He said, "Those who have been forgiven much, love much." Because Jesus had said yes over this poor woman's life and had forgiven her much, she loved Him much. Her love and obedience was a response to, not a prerequisite for, His acceptance. You and I listen for the conditions. We listen for the performance criteria and it's not there. We listen for the "yes, but" and when it's not there we want to build it into the system. We can't believe it because it has been in the heart of the religious system.

f. Religious Performance. We have been well trained to perform for God. Not only has performance been in the family, in the educational system, the social system, and the economic system, but performance has also been in the heart of the religious system. We've been so well trained and so well disciplined to perform for God. On Sunday, we dress up in our "Sunday best." We wash, we scrub, we look nice and clean and proper, and we go to church and perform. We're taught at a very early age to look nice in church, to act nice in church, to give the right answers in Sunday school because we will get a lot of gold stars and a lot of gold stars must mean that we're "in with God." We think that because we have a lot more gold stars than most, our teacher likes us more. Patty and I were in Sunday school, together in high school. She had all these gold stars across the chart, and I would have one here, one there, and occasionally another one. But, because she had more gold stars than I, does that mean that she was more acceptable to her teacher? Somehow, we have a tendency to think that God must be like everybody else and He, too, wants us to perform for His acceptance.

Ben Franklin said, "The problem is not that man has been made in the image of God, but that we have made God in the image of man." We expect God to love as we love, and God's love is as different as day and night from man's love! If your feelings of self-worth are based on how you feel about yourself or how others see you, then you are hooked to the wrong star. You will spend your life climbing the ladder of success, only to find that it was leaning on the wrong building.

Jonathan H. Wilson

John Quincy Adams, who held more political offices than anyone in the history of the United States—President, Senator, Congressman, Master of European Powers, involved in the Revolution, 1812 Civil War—died at the age of 70. He said at the end of his life, "My whole life has been a series of disappointments. I didn't have any success in anything I undertook." Why did he feel that way? There is a television commercial where this guy is talking on the phone and he has something dangling from his finger. It appears that he has had a super glue accident. He is attempting to call the help line to solve this little accident. He's on the phone and is on hold. They tell him that the hold will be for 82 minutes. As the commercial progresses, we find the phone is glued to his ear, the pillow is stuck to his leg, and the cat is stuck to his back. ☺ You probably know of others who do a great job of gluing our faults and mistakes to us. We even do it to ourselves at times.

The world continually reminds us of failures and mistakes, errors, sins, and won't let us live them down. That is why we cannot base our self-esteem on what others think about us. God's love is not that way. Let me quote from I Corinthians 4:3-4, Paul writes, "It matters very little to me what you think of me, even less where I rank in popular opinion. I don't even rank myself. Comparisons in these matters are pointless. I am not aware of anything that would disqualify me from being a good guide for you, but it doesn't mean much. The Master makes that judgment."

Maybe you saw it on the news. It seems that a painting was to be sold for $85. Suddenly someone said, "That looks like a painting from a famous painter." They took a picture of it, examined it and found their suspicion to be true. They took the price tag of $85 off it and put a new price tag of $20,000. They saw its true value.

It is important to know our true worth. An accurate view of yourself comes from an understanding of God's view of who you are. The Lord says to the prophet, Jeremiah, "Before I formed you in the womb, I knew you. Before you were born, I set you apart; I appointed you as a prophet to the nations." When most people think about God speaking to them, they often associate His voice with a guilty conscience. However, the fact is that more often than not the voice of God comes to announce our extraordinary worth to God and His plan to use us in that plan. This personal worth is inseparably tied to the fact that we are made by God, and as this text says, "He brought us to life and shows us off as the Crown of His Creation."

It concerns me when we talk about our self-esteem being equated with our human abilities based on what the world deems attractive at the moment. So let's look at what the Word of God says about this issue.

2. How do we know that God really loves us? James 1:18, says, "We are the crown of all his creatures."

a. "He created me good and perfect." (Verse 17) The phrase in English, "Every good and perfect gift is from above" is even stronger in the Greek. The literal translation is "All good giving and every perfect gift is from above." There are two things to note:

1. The continuous present tense emphasizes the "action" of giving;

2. And, that all His gifts are telion (perfect & complete). In Hebrew, the parallel thought is that the logical, implied sense is that nothing evil can possibly come from above.

b. "He chose me to be in His family." In Verse 16, note that James refers to his readers as brothers and sisters, "Brothers and sisters, don't be misled." Or, stop being deceived. In their miserable flight from Jerusalem and the ongoing persecution, some were not only saying "God is tempting us," but also mouthing the parallel logic that God is not good. Some were, evidentially, saying that if God is so good, why is He allowing them to be persecuted? It is one of Satan's continuous temptations. When he approached Eve in the garden, he suggested that if God really loved her, he would permit her to eat of the forbidden fruit. When Satan approached Jesus in the desert, he raised the same question of hunger, "If your father loves you as you say, why are you hungry?" Stop being deceived; He chose you to be a part of the family.

c. He gives me the freedom to respond. God wants us to respond, but he doesn't give us something that in His infinite wisdom knows is bad for us. He gives us good gifts and wants us to respond, not to lash out at the threat of evil things, but to respond to the love of His goodness. We have all seen, and should know by now, that all people respond better to the expectation of good things and positive reinforcement rather than the punishment of evil. In the world of parenting and teaching and in our parenting classes, Patty and I call it "positive behavior modification." The Lord wants the image of ourselves to be the crowning achievement of His glorious creation.

d. He is consistent; He never changes. (Verse 17) God's goodness "... does not change like shifting shadows." There are no shadows with the Father of light. It is impossible for God to change for the better, because He is perfect. The light of the sun varies as the earth changes, but the sun, itself, is always shining. In other words, God's goodness is always at high noon. Process theology falsely portrays a changing, relativistic God. However, anyone who takes this passage seriously cannot doubt the continuous goodness of God. An old music teacher was once asked in a meeting, "What is the good news today?" The old man without saying a word, walked across the room, picked up a tuning fork and struck it. As the note sounded he said, "That is an A. It is an A today. It was an A 5,000 years ago, and it will be an A 10,000 years from now. The soprano upstairs sings off key, the tenor across the hall is out of tune." He struck the note again and said, "That is A, my friend, and that's the good news today." The good news today and for all eternity is this: God is infinitely good, and He will never change. So, we can quit worrying that His goodness changes like Santa Claus if we've been bad or good; that He is good only if we are good. The light of God's goodness is eternally at high noon.

In his final column in Eternity Magazine, a column he had written for over 20 years, Joe Bayly said, "Since I've shared the severity of God with my readers (speaking of the premature deaths of three of his children), I want to share the goodness of God in this final column. Then he shared God's grace in the lives of each of his four living children. What are especially significant are his final words. "Mary Lou and I are aware that all this represents the grace of God, but also that for ourselves and our children, the road has not ended. Yet, we know that both by his severity and by his goodness, God has shown consistent faithfulness. God is good. He is worthy of all trust and all glory. Amen."

e. He gives me His word as guidance. (Verse 18) Just as human birth requires two parents, so divine birth has two parents: the Word of God and the Spirit of God. The Spirit of God uses the Word of God to bring about the miracle of new birth. He gives us both as sources for guidance. One will not contradict the other. The Spirit of God inspired the Word of God. Of course, the Word of God must feed this new birth in order to keep it alive and well. Alive and well, so that we might be strong to fight the battle of temptation, just as the "Spirit of God" gives you the "Word of God" to give you spiritual birth. He also uses the "Word of God" to give you strength. Spiritual birth, without regular food, starves a person to death. "Man shall not live by bread alone, but by every word that comes out of the mouth of God."

f. "He shows us off as the crown of all his creatures." (Verse 18)

It is only how God feels about us that is of any real consequence in this fickle world. If our Heavenly Father loves us unconditionally, that should be all we need. In the Pan American games, diver Greg Louganis was asked, "How do you cope with stress?" He said, "When I get up on the platform, the second before I dive, I say to myself, 'Even if I blow this dive, my mother will still love me.'" You and I can say, "Even if I blow my life, everything I do, my Heavenly Father will still love me." The question then becomes, "How will we accept the Father's love?"

3. How will I accept the Father's love?

God's love is perhaps best illustrated by perhaps the most famous story in all of literature, certainly in biblical literature. The story is known as the "Prodigal Son," but the true focus is the "Love of the Heavenly Father" and its different effect on two brothers raised in the same family. The scene opens as the younger son screams, "I've had it with this place?" "I want my share of the estate!" "It's a drag around here!" "I'm out of here!" So, the father gave him his share of the estate. The son buys a brand new Hummer, drives to Vegas, and gets an absolutely fabulous penthouse suite on the Strip. He outfits himself, splendidly, and is chillin'. He is the hit of the town. He throws money around like it was water—buying wine, woman, and drugs. He is the last of the big spenders, the check grabber, the big tipper. However, it wasn't long until he had gone through his sizable inheritance. The Hummer was gone, and so

Jonathan H. Wilson

were his fair-weather friends. He had to give up the penthouse suite and take a job as a garbage collector so that he could eat. Finally, he came to his senses when it dawned upon him that things were better at home. So, he decided to go home and he made up a little plan. He was going to make a speech to his father. Jesus tells us that when he got to the house and started up the walk, his father spotted him coming. The father knew that this was his son and his father burst out of the door and ran to greet his son. The son thought as he had learned from his fair-weather friends, that he had to perform to be accepted so he had this little speech all prepared. Suddenly he looks up and there is this old, white-haired man, running down the walk with his arms wide open and this gigantic smile on his face and they embraced. The boy was so conditioned that his self-esteem depended on his performance that he couldn't recognize that there were no conditions. He pushed back his father and said, "Father, I have sinned against you and against heaven and earth." He never got beyond that point because his father threw his arms around him and hugged him and kissed him. He called his servants to get his best suit, his best shoes, and he took the signet right off his finger and put it on the boy's finger symbolizing that he was his son. Then, he sent for the fatted calf, sent it to the killing floor and had the barbecue of all barbecues with everyone invited to the biggest party ever seen. It took the boy a long time to realize that the father really loved him, unworthy as he was; and that because the Heavenly Father loved him unconditionally, he was worthy. When Jesus talks about the father in the story, and the way that he welcomed home his son, he was talking about the unconditional love of God. He was saying to the boy, "Yes, you've blown it; that is true. Your performance has not been worthy by the world's standards. You are not worthy, but I love you and I want you home." Many people wish that the parable would end there, but it doesn't. The prodigal has an elder brother and as the elder brother viewed the situation he was not too thrilled about the whole thing. One Sunday school teacher was telling this story to her class and she reached an eloquent climax. She said, "In the midst of all the joy and excitement, there was one to whom the prodigal's return had no happiness, one to whom the feast meant not good times and rapture, but bitterness. There was one who hated the thought of attending the feast." She looked around the class and she said, "Can you tell me who that was?" One sad

The Good News About Hard Times

little boy in the back stood up and said, "The fatted calf." ☺ No, it was the elder brother. The elder brother was walking through the fields and he said to the servant, Hey, what s with the hard rock up at the house? Haven t you heard? Junior is home and they are throwing a huge barbecue. The elder brother gets angry at that point and he said, Tell my father I am not coming. His father later came out of the house beckoning to the servant. The father said, What is wrong? The elder son said, What s wrong! When did you hire Lawrence Welk for my friends and me? When did you throw a barbecue for me? The father responds, My goodness boy, everything I have is yours. You don t even have to ask for it. The point I believe Jesus was making was that the older brother doesn t realize that for his younger brother a spring of water had been sprung from a rock of desperation. However, for him, a quiet river of water had ever flowed, but he had failed to tap into it because he felt that by his own merit he would measure up. That is the only thing that is wrong with the elder brother. His self-esteem was based on his performance. He thinks he is righteous. He doesn t recognize that he has as much need for the forgiving, unconditional love and pardon of God as does the prodigal son. The tragedy of the story is that one boy sees his life fall, knows his performance is unworthy, and then comes back accepting the invitation to the party. The elder brother had been misled my accepting the world s values. He thinks he doesn t need it and does not open himself to the unconditional love and acceptance of God. You might say, Jon, that sounds really great, but what about the righteousness of God? What about the law of God? What about the commandments of God? Hasn t He given us the law and aren t we called to measure up to it? What about the judgment and the wrath of God? How can you say there are no conditions we are supposed to fulfill?" That is right. God is Holy. The law is absolute and the law stands. You and I are called to measure up. That is where we get into the heart of the issue. God has His "Yes, but..." however we haven't' measured up and God, in His infinite love and mercy, knows that we will never measure up and has come to us in Jesus Christ. Christ has measured up for us. That is what Easter is all about? Jesus Christ has gone to the cross. He has allowed Himself to be nailed there and to die there. He has taken upon His sinless self, our inadequate performance that stands against us. We haven't measured up and will never be acceptable to God on the basis of our performance. Even if we were all Mother Teressas! James is saying, "Don't be misled, my dear friends, by the world. God loves you, not based on your performance, but because you are the "crowning achievement of his incredible creation." Society and Satan have misled us to believe that we must perform to be worthy. However, if we are secure in the unchanging goodness and love of our Heavenly Father, who runs out to greet us even when we have "blown it" badly, there is never any reason to despair. Do you know that Jesus? There was a young man who grew up in a church where he was taught that ritual and good works would help him to be accepted by God. One day he was introduced to the unconditional acceptance of God that salvation is based on faith alone. On the basis of understanding and the goodness of God, he committed his life to the Lord in gratitude. Then he made a very significant statement. He said, "I always knew that I needed Jesus but I never learned until today that He was enough." Do you know that Jesus? Jesus Christ is here today and He loves you with an infinite love. He has done everything possible that He can do for you and He values you with an infinite value. He has made you in His own image and redeemed you with His own blood. He chose you to be a part of his "family." He created you good and perfect. You are His crowning achievement! The only question is, will you accept it? The door to the party is open; we have not been shut out. There are a lot of you here today who are estranged from loved ones and you don't really know that you are loved there. You are frustrated and guilty about your own inability to measure up to the misleading standards of our culture or even to your own expectations.

Jesus Christ came to set you free. You see, that is why He was so misunderstood. That is why He was finally put to death. He came into a world of performers and He didn't force anybody to perform. He came into a world of lonely, frustrated, guilty people and He was the only one who had to perform. Remember the woman who washed his feet? Jesus said, "Those who have forgiven much, love much."

The crowd may be roaring their approval of the good deeds you have done. Or, the crowd may think you are worthless, but it doesn't matter what the crowd thinks. The only thing that really matters is what God thinks about you. Like the prodigal son's father, He stands

The Good News About Hard Times

with open arms waiting for us to come home from the far country—waiting for us to come to our senses.

How will you accept the Father's love? As the prodigal son, or as the elder brother? RSVP, are you coming to the party or not? No decision is a decision.

{"In the Bible, Anger is part of a climatic order of emotions. When we understand the sequence, we can be much more effective in handling anger".

Ephesians. 4:30, "let bitterness and wrath and anger and clamor and slander be put away from you with all malice"}

"Dialogues of the Deaf"

"A Greek word study you should never forget"

Book of James - chapter 6

James 1:19-21

Some years ago, a young man approached Socrates to ask the philosopher to teach him the gift of oratory. His request was then followed by an incessant stream of words until, finally, Socrates placed his hand over the young man's mouth and said, "Young man, I will have to charge you a double fee." When the young man asked why, Socrates replied, "I will have to charge you two sciences. First, how to listen, and then how to speak." I thought of that as we got into today's passage, because communication is not really complete until both listening and speaking has happened. I think that is one of the things that James is getting at.

Many years ago, Dr. Paul Tournier, a theologian and counselor wrote the following, the source of the title of today's message. It is very appropriate when we think of the conversations that are going on in the world today, whether it is NATO, the United Nations, or the Security Council. "Listen to the conversations of the world between nations as well as between couples. They are for the most part, dialogues of the deaf." It seems that dialogues of the deaf appropriately fits what has been going on in our world. Billions and billions of words are being exchanged every second, but only fractions are heard. Conversations without reception! Why is it that we have such a difficult time listening? There are lots of reasons. Sometimes people are so self consumed that they cannot listen to what someone else is saying; others are so intent on what they are going to say next that they don't hear a word that is being said. We ask a question and instead of listening for the answer, we are thinking of our next question. Listening to someone else is very difficult.

James, the brother of Jesus, understood the implications of the inability to listen and of the huge consequences. This is certainly one of the reasons that he wrote so much about it in the Letter of James, specifically Chapter One, Verses 19-21.

Jonathan H. Wilson

1. Problem: "My beloved brethren..." (Verse 19a) He starts out by saying, "My beloved brethren..." Here, James was talking to believers in the early church. "My brethren" is a term of endearment, a phrase of tenderness. He is addressing those Christians in the early church whose attitudes are disrupting the fellowship of the body of Christ. He was pointing out that many of their problems were caused by those who were not listening to God's word, nor to each other.

Pastor Tim Byrd writes, "The greatest cause of disturbances in the church do not come from those on the outside, but Christians with bad attitudes who do not truly hear God's word." James points out three indicators that God's word has been received.

2. Three evidences of truly hearing God's word

a. "Be quick to listen." (Verse 19b) If you were to look at that in the Greek, it would be the present active imperative, i.e., a continuous command. Not something we do once and it is over. We continue to do it over and over again. We keep at it; it isn't something we do at a selected moment. Always, continue to be quick to listen.

b. "Be slow to speak." (Verse 19c) James is encouraging the believers to think before they speak. The ancient Rabbis had a phrase, "Men have two ears and one tongue that they should hear more than they speak. The ears are always open, ever ready to receive instruction; but the tongue is surrounded by a double row of teeth to hedge it in and keep it within proper bounds." If you have, as have only opened my mouth at times to change feet, this counsel rings true. You never have to take back, something that you don't say. Our natural tendency is to be slow to hear, and quick to speak which James would identify as faulty listening. Because of faulty listening, we don't fully understand and therefore we are quick to jump to the wrong conclusions, quick to judge, and quick to say the worst. So, naturally, we pronounce opinions and verdicts on every situation regardless of knowledge of the full facts. But, we need to keep in mind that James' saying, "Be slow to speak," is not an option. It is an ongoing command.

c. "Be slow to get angry." (Verse 19d) This is a third evidence of truly hearing God's word as a person who is slow to get angry. Proverbs

The Good News About Hard Times

19:11 says, "Good sense makes a person slow to anger." James is saying that anger should always be handled with a response interval or a conscious delay that allows evidence and facts to be separated from emotion. A pause of understanding allows everything to be put into proper perspective and the response to be appropriate to the offense. "Be slow to anger" means that the instant my temperature begins to rise, I am automatically to put my response mechanism in neutral until I have the opportunity to think it through completely, the implications and consequences. Some might call that a "strategic delay." It is almost impossible to think and talk, rationally, when you are angry.

This reminds me of the woman that Chuck Swindoll reports about on Internet who was attacked in her car.

Linda Burnett, of San Diedo, Ca. went to a nearby supermarket to pick up some groceries. Some people noticed her sitting in her car with the car windows and her eyes closed, with both hands behind the her head. A customer at the store became concerned and went over to the car. He noted that Linda's eyes were now open, and she looked quite odd. He asked her if she was okay, and Linda replied that "NO" she'd been shot in the back of the head and had been holding her brains in for over an hour. The concerned spectator called the paramedics who broke into the car. When they finally got in, they found that Linda had a wad of bread dough on the back of her head. A Pillsbury biscuit canister had exploded from the heat in the back seat, making a loud sound like a gunshot. The wad of dough had hit her head and when she reached back to find out what it was, she felt the brisket dough and thought it was her brains. She had initially passed out, but quickly recovered and tried to hold her brains in for over an hour until someone noticed and came to her aid.

The AP headline was "Killer Biscuits Wanted for Attempted Murder."

Sometimes we have to take that brain to kind of hold our thoughts in—delayed reaction. Sometimes it means sitting down and writing a letter and praying about whether to send it. I think that a lot of people get into trouble because they don't really understand the process, the biblical sequence of anger.

3. Understanding anger. In the Bible, anger is part of a climatic order of emotions. When we understand that sequence, we can be much more effective in handling anger. In Ephesians 4:30, a key passage, Paul writes, "Let all bitterness and wrath and anger and clamor and slander be put away from you with all malice." There is nothing arbitrary about the order in which Paul used them in this verse. They are in the climatic order.

Bitterness. Bitterness is an inner resentment due to something distasteful. It is the root cause of other words in that sequence. In Hebrews 12:15, we are told "Do not let the root of bitterness grow up inside you." Bitterness is often at the root of many emotional problems. If bitterness is not dealt with effectively, it leads to wrath.

Wrath. Wrath in the Greek means, "internal boiling." It is an inner rage that makes our very insides burn. That is when a person becomes red-faced, ready to explode.

Anger. Anger is an external outburst. The Greek tells us that anger is the first external outburst after much repression or suppression. Often, this is when we see the emotional sequence for the first time. Like that biscuit, it explodes through the surface. Anger is the flaring up of a temper as a result of bitterness, of unresolved wrath when it breaks through the surface.

Clamor. The Greek for the word means a "loud, verbal, self-assertion of an angry person who wants to be sure that everyone hears their grievance." This is where angry bickering may take place. If not dealt with effectively, it may lead to slander.

Slander. Slander is abusive speaking. The Greek word here is familiar to everyone. It is the word "blasphemy," a word often used in the Bible for "speaking against God." It is also a word that is used to speak against our fellow man or against someone in your family. Often it begins with a shot to the hot button, questioning a person's integrity, etc. This often leads to shouting matches that quickly turn into insulting sessions where family heritage is questioned. As the level increases, locker room vocabulary is often plentifully employed and those involved verbally abuse one another in every way under the sun. If progression continues, unchecked, there is yet another level.

The Good News About Hard Times

Malice. Malice is wishing or doing evil to others or ourselves. Malice indicates evil thoughts, thoughts of wishing evil upon someone. In many places in the Bible, it is often fueled by jealousy. However, malice doesn't always stop there. If the root of bitterness continues to grow through these six states without being resolved, malice can result in bodily injury or assault either to one's self, which we call "suicide," or if fatal to another, we call it "murder." Do you see the climatic order of these words? That is why the writer of Hebrews writes, "See to it that no root of bitterness springs up and causes trouble, and by it many become defiled." Once we understand anger as part of a sequence in the Bible, it then becomes easier with which to deal and control. Let's learn how to control anger.

Controlling Anger.

Realize the cost. (Verse 21) James says, "Lay aside..." This means to take off or shed. It implies getting rid of something that is not useful or is costly. James says, "Get rid of all filthiness and overflow of wickedness." The word, "filthiness" is a medical term that refers to wax in the ears. Just as the excess of wax in the ears keeps us from hearing properly, so filthiness in our lives keeps us from hearing God's true word, properly. James says if we have the filthiness of sin in our lives, it will block the hearing of God, the true meaning of God's word. Then James takes it a step further. He says, "Receive with humbleness the implanted word." It must be received. Some people have heard the word of God for years, but have never really received it. James says to receive it, we must have a humble, teachable spirit. James continues, "When the blockage of sin is removed from our lives and we hear it with humility, when we are willing to hear our faults and recognize our sin, then and only then can we begin to be shaped and molded by the doctrines and teachings of God's word to bear fruit." This is James' consistent theme—talk is cheap, but it is the fruit in a person's life that is outward proof that Christ is in their heart. How do you know that an orange tree is an orange tree? By seeing its fruit! It is when the word of God is humbly received, not just heard, that it is able to save your soul.

William McDonald writes of this verse: "The word of God is the instrument God used in the new birth. He uses it in not only saving our soul from the penalty of sin, but also from its power as well.

Jonathan H. Wilson

He uses it in saving us not only from damnation in eternity, but also from damage in this life." What kind of damage? James has been talking about the damage of anger. Does anger get us into trouble? Is the sky, blue? "Anger is one letter away from danger." The Bible is very specific about the damage done by uncontrolled anger. Listen to these: Proverbs 29:22 says, "A hot-tempered man starts fights and gets into all kinds of trouble." Proverbs 15:18, "Hot tempers cause arguments." Proverbs 14:29, "Anger causes mistakes." Proverbs 14:17, "People with hot tempers do foolish things." Proverbs 11:29, "The fool who provokes his family to anger and resentment will finally have nothing worthwhile left." The person with uncontrolled anger has the potential to divide a family and end up with nothing of value left. In other words, when you lose your temper, you are always going to lose out. That is why James says what he does in Verse 21.

Reflect, don't react. (Verse 19) James begins this discussion with the words: "My dear brothers, take note of this..." He is emphasizing the importance of taking notes and thinking about what he is about to say. Then, he talks about the implications of not listening, of speaking off the top of one's head. Proverbs 29:11 says, "A stupid man gives free reign in his anger. A wise man waits and lets it grow cool." To be cool in today's language, "A wise man waits and chills out." Chill out before you put your foot in your mouth. The point of this and other Scriptures is that anger should be dealt with deliberately. "Be slow to anger." Proverbs 19:11 says, "Good sense makes a person slow to anger." Anger should be handled with a reaction interval—a conscious delay that allows evidence and facts to be separated from emotion. Call it a "pause of understanding" that allows time for things to be put into proper perspective and the response to be appropriate to the problem. Having a "reaction interval" or a "reflection interval" means that the instant you feel your temperature begin to rise, you automatically put your "response mechanism" into neutral until you have the opportunity to think it through completely. Think through the consequences of your reaction. Someone wiser than I once said, "Speak when you are angry and you'll have made the greatest "speech" you will ever regret." I would add—write and send a letter or an E-mail when you are angry and you will have written the greatest letter or E-mail you will ever regret. You see, it is almost impossible to talk or to think rationally about problems in the heat of anger. I am not

The Good News About Hard Times

talking about repressing anger for weeks, months, or years. When you swallow your anger, your stomach keeps score. It will come out somewhere on your body—ulcers, and a whole series of problems. When there is "reaction energy" it needs to go somewhere and if not directed elsewhere sugar pours into your system creating energy—blood pressure increases, some say up to 100 points; heart beat increases to 220 or higher. Dr. Wallace Ellerbrook said in a newspaper interview, that when checking coronary victims he finds that they were either very depressed or very angry just before the coronary. A study of Navy Cadets showed that their cholesterol levels soared 140-165 to 400-650 as a result of rising anxiety and anger. When we are angry, additional adrenaline is released, muscles tighten up, ulcers form in the stomach, gastrointestinal systems react, and we have difficulty in swallowing, nausea, vomiting, and constipation; and, most common cause of ulcerative colitis is repressed anger. People are more accident prone on the freeway when angry. We have all had moments when we said something and then five minutes later we thought, "Oh, I wish I'd never said that! That is why James is implying in "slow to anger" that we need that reaction interval.

Relate wisely. James, in Verse 2, says he is writing to all the people who were dispersed among the nations. This letter was not sent out bulk mailing. It was one letter that was copied and recopied, and shared and circulated among people of like mind. The reading of the letter calls them together; he calls them "My brothers..." In controlling anger, watch with whom you associate. Proverbs 22:24-25 says, "Do not make friends with a hot-tempered person. Do not associate with one easily angered, or you may learn his ways and get yourself ensnared." You see, anger is contagious. It is infectious, highly infectious. It is a learned behavior pattern. We learn how to blow up by watching other people blow up. We see it every night on TV in sports highlights. The coach blows up in the game and pretty soon the players are following suit. You handle pressure the way you see it handled. The Proverbs writer says, "Don't hang around with that kind of people because if you do, you will find yourself becoming an increasingly angry person." If you are a hothead, think about it. Do you find that certain people avoid being around you? What will it benefit you to steer clear of hotheads and keep your cool? It is a great benefit. St. Justin wrote, "Keep cool and you rule the world." Nobody wants a hothead

Jonathan H. Wilson

in charge. We want the "cool one" in charge. Those who apply these biblical principles to control anger will find themselves in positions of leadership and respect. Angry, reactionary people are insecure people. Somebody or something threatens them. When they feel threatened, they get angry. Those who don't control their emotions through Christ's presence and power, may see their lives fall apart, again and again, like the great athlete (like a Darryl Strawberry) who has great talent but who will spend much of his life in jail. The hot-tempered are passed over for promotions and they wonder why—because they have not learned control. They have not learned to relate wisely.

Release appropriately. Ephesians 4:15, "There are right ways and wrong ways to release your anger." Some psychologists teach their clients that you've got this bucket full of anger in your life and if you'll just dump out the bucket it will be all empty and everything will be all right and fantastic and happy. They call it "ventilation" therapy. Others call it the "primal scream dumping." If I can just scream out my anger then all things that were done wrong to me while growing up will be fine. There is one good way to express anger. Why do you think so many people play golf? Technically, it is "primal hitting" therapy, a tension release. Here is how it works. Go out to the golf course, take a golf ball, name that golf ball, "Ralph." Tee "Ralph" up, get out your Big Bertha, line up old "Ralph" to take a long hit on a short tee—right into the river, or into the woods. Hasta la vista baby! Or you say, "See you later, Baby!" That is almost like getting saved all over again. Some of the finest golf shots I have ever made in my life involved sending "Ralph" into the river, or into the ocean, or bounding on those rocks, or clanking against some trees. There's a therapy about hitting old "Ralph" and watching him disappear. There's only one problem with that—it doesn't work because we don't have a bucket of anger in our life—we've got an anger factory. This factory doesn't get empty; it just produces more and more anger. Study after study confirms what the Bible has always taught, that aggression causes more aggression. One hard foul leads to another hard foul. Anger causes more anger. Outbursts lead to other outbursts. It is a growing crescendo. Abusive behavior leads to more abuse; and if you become angry, it just leads to more anger until it becomes a pattern within your life. The Apostle Paul talks clearly about how to release it appropriately. Ephesians 4:15 states, "We are to speak the truth in love." The meaning in the Greek is that "we are to speak the truth in such a way that our relationship is cemented together better than before." Speak the truth in a loving way! Being totally blunt and letting it all hang out does not build relationships. By editing our feelings we are taking the reaction energy produced by the anger and turning it into something useful which will build the relationship. Controlled, focused reaction energy used in a positive way is greatly respected.

In Steven Covey's book, The Seven Habits of Highly Effective People, he writes, "Highly effective people do not blame circumstances, conditions or conditioning for their behavior. Their behavior is based on values, not feelings. He defines the word "responsibility" as "response-ability," the ability to choose your response.

Reprogram by the Word. (Verse 21b) James says there is stuff to get rid of and stuff to accept. "Get rid of moral filth and evil." G.I.G.O—Garbage In, Garbage Out. Replace it with the word of God in you. Romans 12:2 says, "Be transformed by the renewing of your mind." Note that renewing is a process that doesn't happen over night. Have you ever noticed a "For Sale" sign in your neighborhood? Then, it's gone—something has happened! Then you see signs of change everywhere. Old is pulled down and fresh new fences, new glass, room additions, and slowly but slowly the place is renewed. In Christian life, a new owner moves into our hearts, slowly begins to make all things new in the process. If you have had a habitual pattern of dealing with anger in an inappropriate way, then you're going to need to practice these over a long term to allow Christ to transform your lifestyle, from one of anger to one of love and patience. Did Paul say, in Romans 12:2, that we are transformed by making New Year's resolutions? Not at all! We are not transformed by New Year's Resolutions; we are transformed by the way we think and that is transformed by Christ in our hearts. The Bible makes it very clear that the way you think determines the way you feel and the way you feel determines the way you act. If I am angry, it is because I feel angry and if I feel angry it is because I am choosing to think angry thoughts. I am not choosing to think like Christ. If you want to change your behavior or your feelings, you have got to change the way you think—to begin thinking like Christ, to reprogram your computer. Your beliefs control your behavior; therefore, you have to start reprogramming your mind. My friends, almost everything in our

Jonathan H. Wilson

society teaches us to express anger in inappropriate ways. Yell at someone, sue someone, beat up someone, shoot him or her—get even! Watch TV some night and observe the inappropriate ways they teach our society to handle anger. Take a poll some night as to how many stories on the evening news have to do with the inappropriate use of anger. War, the threat of war, the angry wife who runs over her husband and is now going to jail for 20 years; two brothers mad at their mother, so they brutally kill her in the same way they saw on a TV program. Patience and love don't sell. Television teaches us in program after program how to solve our problems by getting angry. My favorite program some years ago, when I had time to watch TV, was McIver. He solved all his problems without ever using a gun, without violence. However, that would be too slow and boring, today. Now, most programs seem to be "Get angry, blow them up!" "Get angry, cuss them out." "Get revenge." We are programmed, over and over again, to act out our anger in inappropriate ways.

There is a comparatively tame and humorous way of handling anger in the movie, "Fried Green Tomatoes." An elderly woman is waiting patiently for a parking space at a shopping center, but when the car that she is waiting for pulls out, two young girls zip right in front of her in their sports convertible, taking the parking spot. She leaned out the window and said, "Girls! I've been waiting for that parking spot!" As they got out and went into the store they yelled, "Sorry, lady, but that's what you can do when you're young and quick." Well, she backs up her big car and puts it in gear, puts the pedal to the metal, and smashed this convertible into a pile of junk. The girls run back to what was left of their convertible and scream at her, to which she replies, "Girls that's what you can do when you're old and rich!" So, we need to be reprogrammed through the revival of our minds. Rely on God. (Verse 20) (Genesis 50:20) Verse 20 says, "Man's anger does not bring about the righteousness of God." But God can. Remember the Genesis 50:20 principle, "Even what man intended for evil, God can use for good." We must rely on the total Sovereignty of God to work everything out. John Wesley once said, "I've never known anxiety for any longer than 15 minutes because when I get worried, I just envision God sitting on the throne governing over the affairs of all creation and I know all things will be well."

Obviously, anger in itself is not a sin. Paul wrote in Ephesians 4:26, "Be angry but do not sin." Jesus was angry but He never sinned.

Think of anger as "reaction energy." How can you challenge it for positive gain? Whether it is a sin is determined by what you do with it.

Aristotle once said, "Anyone can be angry, that is easy, but to be angry with the right person, to the right degree, at the right time, for the right purpose, and in the right way, that is not easy."

{"The Bible is a book of Blessings, promising comfort, strength, hope, wisdom, joy, power and purpose. But just be Because you have a Bible doesn't mean you are going to benefit from it. Our Life Coach gives us steps for receiving Gods Blessings"

Ephesians. 4:30, "let bitterness and wrath and anger and clamor and slander be put away from you with all malice"}

"Bible study without application is an abomination"

Book of James, Chapter 7

James 1:19-27

Matthew 13:1-8; 18-23

In America, Bibles are everywhere. You find them in bookstores, grocery stores, and everywhere in motel rooms. I have a program on my computer that has 42 different translations and interpretations of the Bible, including Greek and Hebrew. Every year, about 500 million Bibles are sold in America. Not only is it the number one best seller of all time, but it is the number one best seller every year.

My understanding is that last year there were published 18,000 language portions of the Scripture. We are glutted with the word of God around our country. Turn on the car radio or watch television and you will hear people talking about the Word of God and its implications. Yet, millions of people miss the blessings of the Bible.

Why? Because the blessing of God's Word is not automatic. The Bible is a book of blessings, promising comfort, strength, hope, wisdom, joy, power, and purpose. However just because you have a Bible doesn't mean that you are going to benefit from it. James gives us some key ideas about how to receive its blessing.

James, Verse 25, "The man who looks intently into the perfect law that gives freedom and continues to do this, not forgetting what he has heard but doing it, he will be blessed in what he does." The Bible is called the "perfect word" because it points out our sin and then gives us our opportunity to ask for God's forgiveness. James gives us the following steps for receiving the blessings of the Bible.

I. "I must accept God's word...accept the Word planted in you." Verse 21. Here, James completes his two-part command regarding receiving God's word. The first is a negative; the second is a positive. The negative is that he has just said to get rid of the moral filth and evil that is so prevalent. James says that unwillingness to listen, a sinful tongue, and unrighteous anger are moral evils. If you are slow to hear God's word, quick to speak, and quick to anger, we have not done the spiritual house cleaning necessary to receive God's blessing. If we want to receive and benefit from God's word, we must toss out the sins that have been revealed to us and open ourselves to receive God's word. Once we have done that, we are ready for God's positive command, "Humbly receive God's word implanted in you, which can save you."

II. "I must reflect on God's word...it is like a mirror." (Verses 22-25) The main purpose of owning a mirror, God's perfect law, the Bible, is to be able to see yourself clearly and to make yourself as clean and neat as possible.

a. Look intently. When we look intently into the mirror of God's word, we see ourselves as we truly are. Have you ever seen one of those computer-generated posters they have everywhere now? On the front they have a collage of images, but you don't see the hidden picture underneath by just walking by and glancing at it. You must stop, linger, stare, and study and that is how it is with God's word. Any time you read God's word there is value in just reading it. However, if you really want to go deep in your relationship with Him, if you want deep blessings, you have got to stop and linger and study. As we do so, we begin to internalize the truths of the Bible. God begins to shape and mold and change our lives when we begin to do what God says to do. As that word of God begins to seep down into our minds and hearts, we begin to be renewed and our perspective begins to change. We begin to make decisions differently as we see things from God's point of view.

b. Look continuously, "...and continue to do so..." Looking at ourselves in the mirror of God's word is not a one-time thing. It is not merely a glance. A cursory reading of the Bible never reveals our deepest needs. It is like the difference between a candid photo and a X-ray. One of the things that is painfully true about mirrors is that they are brutally honest. They reveal the painful truth. Reality is staring you in the face. However the point of the mirror is not just to reveal reality, but to show us what needs to be done. It accurately diagnoses us, but it also accurately prescribes a remedy and a solution.

c. Not forgetting "...not forgetting..." Another mistake we make is looking in the mirror and forgetting what we see.

III. "I must receive the word." (Verse 21) The word "accept" in the Greek is a hospitality term, which literally means, "to welcome," "come on in." If we are going to be blessed by the word of God, we must welcome the Word into our lives. James gives us an illustration. He says it is planted our hearts. He gives the illustration of a garden and seed. Constantly, throughout the Bible, it compares itself to the seed. The word of God is always the seed in all the illustrations in the Bible. In fact, Jesus told an entire parable about it as read in today's opening Scripture. The word of God is the seed that is planted in our bodies. How is it that you can take two seeds, exactly the same, put them in different locations and get two different crops in fruitfulness? One soil is prepared; the other is not. One is receptive; the other is not. How is it that you can take two people and put them in the same service and hear the same message? One person is blessed by it, and the other says he didn't get anything out of it. One heart is prepared for worship and the other was not. The parable shows us why this happens. The parable in Matthew 13 shows us why this happens. It has often been called the "Parable of the Sower," but the title misses the point. The focus is not on the sower. It is not on the seed. The focus is on the receptivity of the soil; that is, how we respond to the word of God. It would better be called the "Parable of the Soils." This story was actually used by Jesus as an illustration of a story with many points. First, we need to understand three major points:

(1) Who is the Sower? The Sower is anyone who is sharing the Word of God, clearly. Paul says in Colossians 4, "Pray for us too, that God may open the door for our message so that we may proclaim the mystery of Christ, for which I am in chains. Pray that I may proclaim it clearly..." It has always been my goal to present the word of God, clearly and simply. A worker asked for a pay raise and got this note back from his boss: "Because of the fluctuation predisposition of your positions' productivity capacity as juxtaposed to standard forms, it would be momentarily injurious to advocate your requested increment." The puzzled worker went right to his boss and said, "If this is about my pay raise, I don't get it." "That right," the supervisor said. If I preached like that supervisor talked, you would walk, and I wouldn't blame you. I try very hard to make my messages as clear as possible. A "sower" is anyone who shares the word of God, clearly.

Jonathan H. Wilson

(2) What is the seed? Verse 14 simply says, "The sower sows the word," i.e., the seed is the Word of God. That is simple enough.

(3) What is the soil? This is what the parable is all about. The four kinds of soil are the four ways that we receive the Word of God:

(a) The closed mind. Verse 5, "Some seed fell along the path and it was trampled and the birds at it up." In Palestine, the common ground was divided into long, narrow strips, which each man could cultivate as he wished. There were no fences or walls, but between each was a narrow ribbon of ground about three feet across. This was beaten hard by passersby who used it as a sidewalk. It was a hard path. It became compacted like cement. As he sows the seed, some of it falls on this hardened path. It can't penetrate. It can't get rooted; it doesn't sprout. The Bible says that the birds come along and they eat it and it is gone. The birds represent Satan, according to Jesus. This represents people whose hearts were hardened to the true message of the Gospel. Jesus says the hardened path represented the closed mind. The closed mind says, "I'm not open to what God might want to say." What is it that closes our minds? Jesus talks about the weeds. What is a weed? A weed is anything that I let rob my time with God. It could be a good thing. Anything! How much effort does it take to grow weeds? They grow naturally in my yard. I have many varieties. I don't even have to cultivate them. Weeds are a sign of negligence. When I neglect time with God, when I neglect being in church and reading the Bible, the weeds grow up in my life, my spirtual life gets choked, and my fruitfulness, therefore the blessings, go down the tube.

What are some of the reasons we have a closed mind? Fear, pride, and bitterness.

(1) Fear. We are afraid, somehow, that if we truly hear God's Word that we will lose our fun in life, lose my freedom, my fulfillment. A lot of people just don't tune in to the word of God because they are afraid.

(2) Pride. "I don't need God. I've always done it my way. Besides if I listen to God's word I have to look in the mirror and I have to do something about that. I might have to face up to who I am. I might have to face up to my faults, and I don't want to do that. I don't need

The Good News About Hard Times

God's help. I don't need His advice." Pride is always a smokescreen for insecurity. Always! When I don't want to admit my faults, I deny them. I feel proud, but what I really am is insecure.

(3) Bitterness. There are times when life is tough. We go through painful times and we all experience hurts and sometimes those hurts can harden our hearts. You know of people, right now, that say "I'm going to build a shell around my life and never again am I going to allow anything to hurt me." Bitterness makes you hard and you can't hear what God wants to say to you. The number one reason people don't come to church is because they have been "burned" by another Christian. The tragedy of a hardened heart and a closed mind is that it is barren.

(b) The superficial mind. The second kind of soil represents the superficial mind. Verse 5, "Other seed fell on the shallow soil with rock beneath. This seed began to grow but soon withered and died for lack of moisture." Verse 13, "Those on the rock are the ones who receive the Word with joy when they hear it, but they have no root. The believe for a while, but in the time of testing, they fall away." This is the rocky soil. In Israel, rocky soil doesn't mean soil with a bunch of stones in it. In Israel, there is a thin layer of topsoil across the whole countryside and underneath it is a bedrock of limestone. Plants can sprout very quickly because they're near the surface, but when the heat is on they wither, they die, they fade away. When the wind blows or the storms come, they're gone! The shallow soil is the superficial mind. They get excited but they never let it sink in. How is it that people can attend church week after week and never be changed? Is it because they have no root? The Bible says that they receive it with joy. They are thrilled but not transformed. They jump on the bandwagon and get all motivated but they never let the Word of God penetrate the bedrock of their personality so they're not changed permanently. They are great joiners. They'll volunteer and join at the drop of a hat, but they don't usually come back. The Bible says, "They believe for awhile, but then they forget it." A lot of people start off great—gung-ho—in the Christian life, but there is no depth to their commitment. Like James says, "They look into a mirror and forget." As a result, when problems come, when the heat is on, when the storms of life come, they dry up and blow away. If you don't have any roots when the pressure's on—the heat's on—you are going to dry up and blow away. A tree's strength in a storm is the depth of its roots. Some accept and reject just as quickly. They live on feelings, not convictions. They have a superficial shallow faith, a faith like the skim of dirt on a rock. However, the deep roots are not there, so when the miracles they want don't happen, they wash away in the storm.

(c) The distracted mind. Verse 7, "Other seed fell among the thorns." Other seed fell among thorns [weeds] which grew up with it and choked the plants." Weeds choke out the life of a plant. Verse 14, "The seed that fell among thorns stands for those who hear, but as they go on their way, they are choked by life's worries, riches, and pleasures and they don't mature." How can we be distracted?

(1) First is the preoccupied mind. There are things that crowd in and choke out what God started. In this soil, the Word of God gets into your mind and starts growing, but as it starts growing all the other things come into you life—budgets, bills, career—and choke out the time with God. The seed suffocates. It sprouts but there is no fruit, only because we are preoccupied. The important gets choked by the urgent. God wants us to bear fruit. What kind? Galations 5, "The fruit of the Spirit is love, joy, peace, patience, kindness, goodness, faithfulness, gentleness, and self-control." This is the character of Christ that God wants us to build in our lives, but most people don't have this in their life because of weeds. Why don't we bear fruit? We're too busy. We are preoccupied. We're so involved with the urgent that we don't have time for the important. Our cares are committed to trivia pursuit, things that really don't matter. There is no time for God because there are too many other demands on our life, "Sorry God, I'll do it tomorrow." "Sorry God, you get leftover time, I've got to get to work. I have things on my mind. I've got places to go, people to see, and things to do." Can we be distracted with "busy-ness?" God can't get through because of our preoccupation. Have you ever tried to make a long distance phone call on a holiday, such as Mother's Day? "Sorry, all circuits are busy at this time!" Are your circuits ever too busy for God? "I'm too busy, too preoccupied." A prophet told a parable to King Ahab in I Kings 20:38. He told how during a battle he had been left in charge of a prisoner. He was told that if the prisoner escaped, his own life would be forfeited. However, he allowed his attention to be distracted and the prisoner escaped. His excuse was, "As your servant was busy here and there, he was

The Good News About Hard Times

gone." We're too busy. We get distracted by the urgent and miss the important.

(2) Worries. Verse 22, "The worries of this life...choke it." A book I was reading had a chapter about worry. The chapter was entitled "The Most Popular Form of Suicide is Worry." It stated: "Worry is a slow disease of the mind that cuts the nerve to motivation. The young are made old by it, the old are sent too soon to the grave by it. It kills the appetite, causes insomnia, spoils the taste for living, irritates the disposition, warps the personality, weakens the mind, and saps energy. Students who worry ususally make lower grades; teachers who worry produce neurotic students; management that worries causes unrest among labor. Because of worry, lovers have separated, wars have ripped the world apart. Worry is soul poison, the number one enemy of mankind."

(3) Riches. Verse 22, "...the deceitfulness of wealth chokes the good seed." You can be so busy making a living that you don't make a life. You can be so consumed with making more money that you don't have time for God and the true blessings in life. You don't have time to soak in His word and to bear fruit.

(4) Pleasures. The pleasures of life, such as recreation can take priority over worship and choke out God. I want to have my fun, my hobbies, my golf game, my cabin, my boat, and my Internet time. God, you take a back seat! Even good things that God has given us can keep us from hearing Him. Next is the one that Jesus wants us to be.

(5) The open, receptive mind. Verse 15, "The seed on good soil stands for those with a noble and good heart, who hear the word, retain it, and by persevering produce a crop." Good soil is productive. The good soil is a willing mind. I am willing to do whatever God wants and follow Him completely. James 1:22, "Do not merely listen to the word, and so deceive yourselves. Do what it says!" The word in the Greek for "listen" is also the word used for "auditor." Perhaps you audited a class in school. You took no notes, no credit, no research, and no responsibility. You just listened, with no intention of applying it. We have a lot of auditors in the church. They walk in, hear the word of God, walk out unchanged with no intention of ever being changed. However, James says that in order for our lives to be truly blessed, we must have an open, receptive

mind. The good soil is (1) receptive enough to take the seed in; has depth to allow the seed to let down its roots and draw the food and water it needs, and is pruned from weeds enough not to hinder the growth of the seed. Jesus was saying that the "Word of God" is always good, but its impact depends on the receptivity of the soil—the seriousness with which we hear, understand, and do the word of God.

IV. I must behave God's word. Verses 22-25, "...if you do what it says..." James says that hearing God's word must be followed by obedience. True acceptance of God's word means doing it. Chuck Swindoll writes the following in his book, Improving Your Serve:

Let's pretend that you work for me. In fact, you are my executive assistant in a company that is growing rapidly. I'm the owner and I'm interested in expanding overseas. To pull this off, I make plans to travel abroad and stay there until the new branch office gets established. I make all the arrangements to take my family in the move to Europe for six to eight months, and I leave you in charge of the busy stateside organization. I tell you that I will write you regularly and give you direction and instructions. I leave you and you stay. Months pass. A flow of letters are mailed from Europe and received by you at the national headquarters. I spell out all my expectations. Finally, I return. Soon after my arrival I drive down to the office. I am stunned! Grass and weeds have grown up high. A few windows along the street are broken. I walk into the receptionist's room and she is doing her nails, chewing gum, and listening to her favorite disco station. I look around and notice the wastebaskets are overflowing, the carpet hasn't been vacuumed for weeks, and nobody seems to care that the owner has returned. I ask about your whereabouts and someone in the crowded lounge area points down the hall and yells, "I think he's down there." Disturbed, I move in that direction and bump into you as you are finishing a chess game with our sales manager. I ask you to step into my office (which has been temporarily turned into a television room for watching afternoon soap operas). "What in the world is going on, man?" "What do you mean?" "Well, look at this place! Didn't you get any of my letters?" "Letters? Oh yeah, sure, we got every one of them. As a matter of fact, we have had a "letter study" every Friday night since you left. We even have divided all personnel into small groups and discussed many of the things you wrote. Some of those things were really interesting. You'll be pleased to know that a few of us have actually committed to memory some of your sentences and paragraphs. One or two memorized an entire letter or two! Great stuff those letters!" "Okay, okay, you got my letters; you studied them and meditated on them, discussed and even memorized them. But, what did you do about them?" "Do! Uh, we didn't do anything about them."

Such behavior would be professional suicide! Yet, when we read and study God's word without obeying it, James says (Verse 22) "Do not merely listen to the word, and so deceive yourself. Do what it says." James uses two examples to illustrate what he is getting at—a wrong way and a right way. Verses 23 & 24 explain the wrong approach, "Anyone who listens to the word but does not do what it says, is like a man who looks at his face in a mirror and after looking at himself, goes away and immediately forgets what he looks like." James is saying that God's word is the "mirror." We must look into it and allow it to change us. There is a great delusion out there that says that all we have to do is hear God's word. We hear it and nothing changes. We audit the sermon for mistakes instead of letting it change our lives. James is saying that unless the Word has made a change in our lives, it has not really entered our lives.

Howard Hendricks, author and professor at Dallas Theological Seminary, was one of my mentors. He was a great Bible teacher, indeed, but also he greatly applied God's word. You never left his Bible study or sermon without being challenged to apply God's word and let it change your life. At Mount Hermon years ago he said "Bible study without application is an abomination!" This brings us to the apex of James' point. The man described as "doing" the word lives in obedience. This is the right way! He keeps looking in the mirror of God's word, and doing—looking and doing, looking and doing! Biblically, true knowledge demands action. They cannot be separated. James tells us that it is self-deception when we don't let the word of God change us. The test of maturity is not knowledge. The test of maturity is character. A lot of people have great Bible knowledge, but are spiritual midgets. We need to practice it, apply it, and put it in our lives.

V. I will be blessed by God's word. (Verse 25) "...then God will bless you..." James closes his thoughts on this issue with the "be attitude,"

Jonathan H. Wilson

"He will be blessed in what he does." The key to happiness and blessing is doing God's word.

John wrote in John 13:17, "Now that you know these things, you will be blessed if you do them." Bob Buford has written a wonderful book called, Halftime, where he writes his seven goals for the second half of his life. His seventh goal is "I am committed to the practice of altruistic egoism." Are you familiar with that term? He defines "altruistic egoism" as the commitment to gaining personal satisfaction by helping others.

Occasionally, I hear a story of how the seed from this pulpit is shared around the world on tapes, even in places in the world where it is against the law to listen to Christian tapes. To hear that is truly a blessing to my heart. A few weeks ago, I was told by one of our members that these tapes are circulating among doctors on a medical staff in a hospital in the San Fernando Valley. A lady, who can no longer get out of her home, passes them on to her son who listens and passes them on to others in his family. The good seed is finding receptive soil and it blesses my life. Another blessing in my life has been to go and help out at a Christian orphanage in Mexico, sponsored by our Rotary Club; also, to the Home for the Blind in Los Angeles. In Verse 27, James tells us, "Religion that is pure and faultless is to look after orphans and widows in their distress." When we do these things, we are truly doing God's word and not only will the Lord be blessed, but so will those we help. It will be personally rewarding as well.

What are we saying to the Lord? Are we saying to the Lord, "Letters, Lord? Oh yeah, sure we got everyone of them. We have them all around the house. We even have a 'letter study' twice a week. We discuss many of the things you wrote. They were interesting. I've even been memorizing some of your sentences. Great stuff those letters!"

Is the Lord saying to us, "Okay, you got my letters, you had letter studies, but what did you do about them? What are you doing to spread the good seed to receptive people?" Altruistic egoism is the commitment to gaining personal satisfaction by helping others—not just talking, but doing something for others—thereby bearing fruit

The Good News About Hard Times

and thereby receiving the blessing of God. A life mission statement like that changes our entire lives.

James is telling us that if we want to be blessed we must "Read my word, and DO IT!" The end result of blessing God, and blessing others, is that we in turn are tremendously blessed ourselves.

{"Mr. Rogers was the epitome of what James was trying to teach us, that our lives are not for ourselves... life is for service"

James 1:12 "So whenever you speak or whatever you do, remember that you will be judged by the law of love, the law that sets you free. For there will be no mercy for you if you have not been merciful to others. But if you have been merciful, then Gods mercy toward you will win out over His judgement against you."}

"How to Have Successful Relationships"

"Attitudes that God Blesses"

Book of James Series - Chapter 8

James 2:1-13

In our society today, we like to think of ourselves as open-minded and fair. We pride ourselves in believing that we look past externals and avoid making personal judgments of others. Unfortunately, on the basis of externals, this is not usually true, even in the church. I came across a letter that could have been written, if Jesus had evaluated those first disciples the way we evaluate people today:Tim Hansel wrote about this in his book "Eating Problems for breakfast"

Jesus, Son of Joseph
Woodcrafter Carpenter Shop
Nazareth, Galilee

Dear Sir:

Thank you for submitting the resumes of the 12 men you have picked for managerial positions in your new organization. All of them have now taken the battery of tests and we have run them through our computers. It is the staff's opinion that most of your nominees are lacking in background, educational, and vocational aptitude for the type of enterprise you are undertaking. They do not have the team concept. We would suggest that you continue your search for persons with experience and proven capability.

Only one of the candidates shows great potential. He is a man of ability and resourcefulness who meets people well and has a keen business mind. He has contacts in high places and is highly motivated, ambitious, and responsible. We recommend Judas Iscariot as your controller and right-hand man.

We wish you every success in your new venture.

Sincerely yours
Jordan Management Consultants
Jerusalem, Judea

Jonathan H. Wilson

Isn't that just the way it is today? We look at people by what they have and how they can help us, rather than what is in their heart. James tells us in 2:1 that we are not to show favoritism. That means that we are not to look at one person over another because of what they have or how they can benefit us. Biblical scholars say that the language, as well as the context, indicates an actual happening in the early church. All indication is that James, himself, had witnessed favoritism.

To set his point firmly in the minds of the church, he lays before us a picture of a worship service. He tells the story of two men arriving at church at the same time. They are first time visitors, as James says they don't know where to sit. One guy has gold rings and is obviously dripping with gold as a sign of wealth. Literally in the Greek, it says he is "goldfingered." Wasn't there a movie starring James Bond with a similar name? Notice that James does not criticize the guy for being wealthy, he criticizes the members for being partial to him. He doesn't have anything bad to say about trying to look your best; the problems comes when the believers treat you differently.

Be honest, today, if a rich man entered the service and a poor man followed, who would you be more excited to see? If you saw the first man drive up in a Lexus, have on a nice suit and jewelry, would you think to yourself, "Wouldn't it be great if he would pick our church to attend?" My friends, that is favoritism. Considering one person of greater value over another is wrong. To "Mr. Rich Goldfinger," the usher says, "Come up to the best seat in the house, we want you to be comfortable and to be seen by all." To "Mr. Poor Nobody," the usher says, "You can stand over there in the corner or you can sit on the floor." The Greek says, literally, "I want you under my footstool" where I can keep an eye on you. James is telling us not to do that kind of thing, not to show favoritism to those from whom we think we can benefit. Power ties…"Favoritism has many hats." (Verse 1:4) Let's look at a few power ties as a kind of favoritism.

1. Appearance. I didn't see it but I saw enough to make me know I wouldn't want to see it—it's the new reality show, "Who's Hot?" Guys and gals come out stripped down as much as the law allows then strut their bodies while telling the world why they are "hot." Another example, in Friday's USA TODAY was a story about a three-minute dating service. They take cruise ships where you dance or talk with a person for three minutes and then grade them from

The Good News About Hard Times

one-to-ten, based on short face-to-face encounters. The root of the word, "favoritism" comes two different words that mean "to receive" and "to face." It literally means, "to receive somebody's face." James is telling us to receive somebody at face value is simply to judge on external, superficial values. James is saying that we should never treat someone different according to his or her outward appearance. You will misread them every time.

2. Power pockets. (Verses 5-7) We judge people by whether they are rich or poor. Think about the incredible popularity of "Joe Millionaire." Money in a person's pockets makes a big difference. A man called the church and asked if he could speak to the "head hog at the trough." Sure that she had heard correctly, the secretary said, "Sir, if you mean our pastor, you will have to treat him with more respect and ask for the reverend or the pastor. Certainly, I cannot refer to him as the head hog at the trough!" The man responded, "I see, I was planning on giving $10,000 to the building fund." The secretary exclaimed, "Oh my, hold the line, I think the big pig just walked through the door." Power pockets—definitely one kind of favoritism. In 1884 a young man died, and after the funeral his grieving parents decided to establish a memorial to him. With that in mind they met with Dr. Charles Eliot, president of Harvard University. Eliot received the unpretentious couple into his office and asked what he could do for them. After they expressed their desire to fund a memorial, Eliot impatiently said, "Perhaps you have in mind a scholarship." "We were thinking of something more substantial than that, perhaps a building," the woman replied. In a patronizing tone, Eliot brushed aside the idea as being too expensive and the couple departed. The next year, Eliot learned that this plain pair had gone elsewhere and established a $26 million memorial named Leland Stanford Junior University, better known today as Stanford University. This is another example of how wrong it can be to judge people by their appearance. However, appearance and affluence are not the only factors of favoritism. Another is education.

3. Education. (Verses 8-11) When James says don't favor some people more than others, I am sure he had in mind those who seek power by their education. A man or a woman may not be rich, but in many churches if they are pedigreed—with many degrees—regardless of their spiritual qualifications they are told, "We want you to be on the elder board." Some churches will not even look at a pastor unless he or she has a doctorate. Do you know what a

doctorate degree has to do with ministry? Absolutely nothing, zero, nada, zilch! Education has nothing to do with spiritual maturity or leadership. All these factors can lead to favoritism and a sense of elitism. In fact, elitism has been the downfall of many churches. When you study the history of some denominations you find that many began as small, loving fellowships that included everyone, and they grew and grew. Somewhere the success leads to becoming elitist, and then decline often begins. The eighteenth century Church of England became so elitist and unwelcome to the common man that in 1739 John Wesley had to take to graveyards and fields to preach to the common man. Thus was founded the Wesley-Episcopal church. Wesley did not want to cause division, but he saw there was no room in the established church for the common people. One hundred years later, William Booth, a Methodist, noticed that the poor were hardly ever in church. He objected to the fact that the best pews facing the pulpit, with backs and cushions went to those who put the most shillings into the offering plates, while the poor were delegated to back-less pews behind a screen, out of view from the pulpit. He objected and was expelled by the Methodists. He experienced 14 years of poverty before founding the Salvation Army. Discrimination between the attractive and unattractive, the rich and the poor, educated or uneducated, are not the only discrimination the church has to be careful of, just the most obvious. James was saying, "Do not discriminate."

4. Power judgments. (Verses 12-13) Some say, "The clothes make the man." It is not that the clothes make the man, but that the clothes shape our opinion of the man or woman. They also say, "Don't judge a book by its cover," but in reality that is what we do. We make judgments on people by the way they dress, how expensive their clothes or car, the color of their skin, their attractiveness, their wealth, etc. It impresses us. Verse 4 says, "Don't be partial in yourselves, because you judge by false standards," i.e. you will judge without knowing the heart. James says that we are not to judge people, that is God's job. Our job is to minister to the person, not to judge him based on social standings. One of the things that attracted me to this church as pastor was the rich diversity of its people and the sense that everyone is welcome. This is not a status church for the high rollers. We have no "sugar daddies." All are welcome—rich or poor; educated or not educated; nicely dressed or not; employed or unemployed; whatever the ethnic background or nationality. We

The Good News About Hard Times

probably have more nationalities than any church near our size. James was touching on one of the main principles in the Gospel—treat everyone the same. The sad truth is that the church has not always acted this way. In his autobiography, Mahatma Gandhi wrote that during his student days, he read the gospels seriously and considered converting to Christianity. He believed that in the teachings of Jesus, he could find the solution to the caste system that was dividing the people of India. One Sunday he decided to attend services at a local church and to talk to the minister about becoming a Christian. When he entered the sanctuary, however, the usher refused to give him a seat and suggested that he worship with his own people. Gandhi left the church and never returned. He later wrote, "If Christians also have caste systems, I might as well remain a Hindu." That usher's prejudice not only betrayed Jesus, but also turned people away from God. James says that we are to act as those who are going to be judged by the law that gives freedom because judgment without mercy will be shown to anyone who has not been merciful. Mercy triumphs over judgment. While we are to treat people the way that Jesus accepted us, the other side of that is that if we do not show people the same mercy that was shown us, we are rejecting that mercy and we will be judged with the same judgment that we use. If we do not show mercy, we will not receive mercy. It is as simple as that. This applies to how we interact with people from all walks of life, both rich and poor. The story is told of the politician who, after receiving the proofs of a picture to be used for publicity, was very angry with the photographer. He stormed back to the photo studio with these angry words: "This picture does not do me justice!" The photographer replied, "Sir, with a face like yours you don't need justice, what you need is mercy." We are not called to judge one another, we are to be merciful and then we will receive mercy. In essence, James is saying that we are called to a greater way. James says that the primary reason we are not to show favoritism is because it is unloving and we are called to the royal law, the Law of Love.

5. The power of love. (Verse 8) In Verse 8, James calls us to obey Jesus' Royal Law of love, to love your neighbor as yourself. Jesus demonstrated the power of "love without partiality" in the story of the Good Samaritan. One day a lawyer of religion went to Jesus and asked him what he must do to inherit eternal life? Jesus responded with the Royal law, "You must love the Lord your God with all your

Jonathan H. Wilson

heart, soul, strength, and mind, and your neighbor as yourself." The lawyer who wanted to justify his partiality and prejudice asked, "Who is my neighbor?" Jesus then responded with the Parable of the Good Samaritan. (Luke 10:25-37) In this parable, Jesus was showing us a picture of the judgmental attitude without mercy that God does not want us to have. And then, a picture of the kind of nonjudgmental merciful and accepting attitude that God wants us to have towards everyone, especially those that are hurting and/or wounded. A Jewish man was walking from Jerusalem to Jericho when a gang of thieves jumped him, robbed him, and beat him leaving him to die. Let's look at the various attitudes towards the wounded man that demonstrate the power of love.

a. Bandits: an object to exploit. The robbers were people that thought only about their own personal gain. They didn't care who they had to beat up or what they had to do to get what they wanted. They didn't love or have compassion for others; they were those who simply exploited others. If you have ever read the definition of a "borderline personality disorder," I think they would fit. The whole world revolves around them; people are simply objects to be exploited.

b. Priest: A problem to avoid. The good news was that a Jewish priest came walking along. The bad news is that he crossed by on the other side of the road and passed him by. This is the person who is religious but who, as we talked about last week, doesn't allow his beliefs to affect his behavior. He goes to "letter studies" but they don't affect his behavior. At a Princeton seminary some years ago, a professor gave an assignment to thoroughly exegete the parable of the Good Samaritan. When the class was over, the young men returned to their rooms to study the parable in depth. On the next morning, unknown to the students, the professor had planted a fellow student in the bushes by the walkway leading to the class. The student in the bushes was dressed the part of a battered and beaten bum. Ketchup had been spread generously over his clothes to give the appearance of blood. Hurrying to class armed with pages of notes on the Good Samaritan, not a single student stopped to assist the "injured" party. Have you heard the expression, "So heavenly bound, they are no earthly good"?

c. Innkeeper: A customer. The innkeeper's response to the wounded man was minor and simple; he saw him as an opportunity to make some money.

The Good News About Hard Times

d. Temple assistant: An object of curiosity. This temple assistant came over and looked curiously at the beaten man, but then walked to the other side and went about his business. Do you think this would ever happen? Kitty Genovese was brutally attacked as she returned to her apartment late one night. She screamed and shirked as she fought for her life, yelling for 30 minutes, until she was hoarse as she was beaten and abused. Thirty-eight people watched with great curiosity. They watched, doing nothing during the half-hour episode from their window with rapt fascination. Not one so much as picked up a telephone and called the police. Kitty died that night as 38 witnesses watched in curious silence. Now, after these bad examples, Jesus told about the Samaritan.

e. Samaritan: A person to love. Even though there were hostile feelings between the Samaritan and the Jews, the Samaritan felt compassion for the man and he stopped, soothed and bandaged the wounds. He then put the man on his donkey and took him to the inn and covered his expenses until he could return. James 2:13, "For he who shows no mercy will incur judgment without mercy." The key phrase is in Luke 10:33, "When he saw him, he had compassion." Luke 10 fits into James 2 because a seemingly religious priest and Levite passed up a man in need; yet they know the law. Only the Samaritan fulfilled the Royal Law.

f. Jesus: A person worth dying for. Of course, it was Jesus who was telling the story and Jesus in the ultimate act of mercy and love, laid down his life for the wounded, back then and even today. There would be no justice without God's incredible mercy for the wounds of sin. Well, what happens when we translate the Samaritan's love and compassion into the church? I guess it would be an incredibly fantastic church to be filled with good Samaritans who live by the Royal Law.

6. The power of a loving church. How do you have a loving church? There was an article in the paper, "A Loving Connection in Church Growth." Scholarly studies report that more people are drawn to caring facilities. It is talking about how churches grow. "On the basis of a survey of 8,600 people from congregations in 39 different denominations, they measured their love quotient. The institute reports that growing churches are more loving to each other and to visitors than declining churches. Loving churches attract more people regardless of their theology, denomination or location. They

surveyed them and gave them a quotient of 1 to 100. Of the 12 denominations scoring below 65, all of them except 2 were declining. Of the 13 denominations scoring above 65, all were growing in the last 10 years. Most churches that are growing today have learned how to love. A church that loves people is a church that grows. Typically, in analyzing reasons for growth in a church, the focus in the past has been such factors as pastoral leadership, attractiveness of facilities, location, liberal or conservative theology, and evangelical fervor. However, there is increasing evidence that none of these influence a church's growth or decline as significantly as how much love and acceptance people experience when they attend." The number one denomination, the most loving denomination, was the Southern Baptist Convention, "the largest Protestant denomination scoring 74, the highest love quotient, with a growth rate of 16% a year." It is love like that that reaches people. You don't argue people into the Kingdom of Heaven. You love them into the Kingdom of Heaven. How do you do that? Three steps:

(1) Accept everyone. Romans 15:7, "Accept one another just as Christ has accepted you; then God be glorified." Do you know why people have a hard time accepting others? They confuse acceptance with approval. There is a big difference. You can accept someone without approving his or her lifestyle. They may be doing something that is contrary to the Word of God, but you can accept them as a person without approving of the sin in which they are involved. Paul tells us to accept everyone, "Accept one another just as Christ has accepted you; then God be glorified. We are trying to create a community of acceptance. I say, every time we have communion, "The church is a hospital for sinners, not a hotel for saints." If you are perfect, you don't belong here. This is a church for people who don't have it all together. We have every kind of background you can imagine. We have Catholics, Charismatics, Baptists, Episcopalians, Lutherans, Assembly of God, Pentecostals, Evangelical Free, Mormons, and Atheists. It doesn't matter where you have been. What matters is where you are now and if you want to keep on growing in love. If you want to grow more and more like Him every day, you are welcome here. In the essential we have unity. Jesus is Lord. The Bible is God's Word. In the non-essentials we have liberty and in all things we have charity. Acceptance is the key. If we can't get along with everybody here on earth, what makes us think we'll get along together in Heaven. Accept everyone! Life Magazine did a photo

The Good News About Hard Times

essay a few years ago. They took people from all walks of life, from street people to Fortune 500 executives and photographed them each undressed except for a bath towel. The amazing thing is that you could not tell who was who. They all, basically, looked the same. This is the way we come to Jesus, naked with nothing to offer, and it is at that point that Jesus accepts us, from the poorhouse to the penthouse, He accepts us all the same way. He loves us, He forgives us for our faults, He gives us his Holy Spirit, and He lifts us up to be a child of the King of Kings. He calls us to accept people in the same way.

(2) Appreciate everyone. This goes beyond acceptance. Philippians 2:3, "Do nothing from selfish ambition or vain conceit, but in humility consider others better than yourself. Each of you should look not only to your own interest, but also to the interest of others." Appreciate everybody! Find something you can like, not just accept. Tell them so. With some people this may require a little creativity.

(3) Affirm everyone. 1 Thessalonians 5:11, "So encourage one another and build each other up." Give everyone a lift whenever you can. When people stumble, don't criticize. Instead, sympathize. Be an encourager—not a complainer, a condemner, a critical person, a judge. Someone has said, "The church is the only institution in the world that shoots its wounded." Oh Lord, let that not be so! That is not the Royal Law. That is not what the Good Samaritan would do. You can encourage someone just by smiling at them. When we have visitors, remember we only have one chance to make a good impression. Greet people with a big smile and a welcoming handshake. Don't overdo it. I talked with a visitor a few weeks ago that came in and wanted to get a feel of the church. During the greeting time someone saw them as visitors and gave them 20 questions. They felt overwhelmed. There is a delicate balance between being friendly and being nosey. As yourself the question, "Would people come back to the church because of you?" What is God saying to us through James? The church that accepts, appreciates, and affirms people is the church that God blesses. It is not the responsibility of one or two people, but every single person. Nothing can stop the church that is filled with love. It requires an all out effort by every one of us. Everybody needs to contribute to the atmosphere of the church. Like it or not, every person here contributes to the atmosphere of the church, either negatively or positively. If we want to be God's church we want to have a reputation for love. I believe that God is just waiting

for a church to love people unconditionally. Nothing can stop a loving church. If you are a visitor, either long-term or short-term, you are as welcome as one of the charter members of the church. It really doesn't matter what you wear or your economic status; or whether you've been married, never married, or married five times. It doesn't matter what race or nationality you are or whether you are employed or not. You are welcomed here. Acceptance! It is said of the early church, "See how they love one another. By this shall all men know that you are my disciples, that you love one another." You accept, affirm, and appreciate. Lee Iacocca once asked the legendary football coach, Vince Lombardi, what it took to make a winning team. The book, Iacocca, records his answer. "There are a lot of coaches who know the fundamentals and have plenty of discipline but still don't win the game. Then you look for a third ingredient: If you're going to play together as a team, you've got to care for one another. You've got to love one another." That is the difference between mediocrity and greatness. Lombardi said it right. The difference is the feeling of love these guys have for each other. This week, one of TV's greatest personalities said, "Well, it's been a sad day in the neighborhood." I was deeply touched, as I'm sure some of you were this week with the death of Reverend Fred Rogers, a Presbyterian minister, better known as "Mr. Rogers." I heard him and met him when he spoke at the General Assembly of the Presbyterian Church some years ago. He died from stomach cancer at age 74. How many of you have seen Mr. Rogers' neighborhood at one time or another in your life? Anyone remember the phrased he used in every episode? "I like you just the way you are." His TV show was one of the best programs on TV for 35 years. He only took a break from children's TV to go to seminary and become ordained as a Presbyterian minister. He was then commissioned to children's ministry through TV. He won every honor from the Emmy to the Peabody. Four years ago he was elected to the broadcasting Hall of Fame. He did some 900 children's shows, but he intimately talked to you like you were a good friend and really were important to him, and somehow you knew that you were. Important that they were not just words, that he really did care, and that he lived what he taught. Mr. Rogers showed up like clockwork every day at the same time. He always walked in the door with a smile on his face. He took of his jacket and his good shoes and put on those canvas sneakers and an old cardigan sweater. He didn't quote the Bible much, but he taught Biblical values. He taught us to be kind, to be open and without prejudice. He was in my eyes and those of many

The Good News About Hard Times

others the epitome of what James is trying to get into our thick skulls. That is, that our lives are not for ourselves, but one of his terms was that "life is for service." He created a safe neighborhood for children to be themselves and learn the values and lessons of the "good book," and to love your neighbors as yourself. I think that he would desire his beloved Presbyterian Church to create a safe environment for old and new friends. A place where people really loved each other unconditionally as Jesus loved us. I think he would want us to say to each other, in deed if not in words as he said on every program for 35 years, "I like you just the way you are," because Jesus likes me just the way I am and in fact he laid down his life for me—just as I am!

Mr. Rogers' "I like you just the way you are," encouraged children and helped them confront their fears. He had a way of talking as if only one child was there. He assured children that it is natural to get upset and okay to cry, then smile again later on. He said, "Feelings are natural and normal—happy and sad—part of everyone's life." If we were to start every staff meeting thinking of a person who had been a positive influence in our lives—White House, President Clinton, Vice President Gore, Bill Cosby—the message would always be the same, "You are loved just the way you are." It gives us a kind, gentle, warm and fuzzy feeling. To again quote "Mr. Rogers," "It's a beautiful day in the neighborhood, would you be mine? Could you be mine? Won't you be my neighbor?"

If we want to have successful relationships, we should try to live our lives like Jesus. If you need a modern day example, perhaps not perfect but as close as we will see, look at "Mr. Rogers" who took his guidelines from Scripture. Verse 8, "It is good when you truly obey our Lord's Royal command." Also found in Scripture; "Love your neighbor as yourself." Verse 12, "So whenever you speak or whatever you do, remember that you will be judged by the Law of Love, the law that sets you free. For there will be no mercy for you if you have not been merciful to others. But if you have been merciful, then God's mercy toward you will win out over His judgment against you."

Jesus, out of love and mercy, went to the cross to satisfy the judgments against us. How is your judgment-mercy quotient? Have you been judgmental or merciful to others? If you have been judgmental, you have a lot of forgiveness to seek.

{"Paul and James were asking two different questions. Paul was answering the question, 'How do we receive salvation? The answer is not by works, but by faith. James is asking 'How is faith recognized?' And the answer is 'Fruit'!

James 2:4 "Its not just faith, but faith and works"}

"The Road to Success-Reality Faith"

"Many hands make light work"

Book of James - Chapter 9

James 2:14-26

Over the centuries the human race has passed along a lot of wisdom from generation to generation through wise sayings. They are an everyday part of life and we usually use them without thinking. Let's think of a few; I want you to vote on, which of two expressions is the wisest: (a) "Look before you leap" (b) "He who hesitates is lost." Or, "Out of sight, out of mind" (b) "Absence makes the heart grow fonder." Which ones, in general, do you think are the best choices for a philosophy by which to live your life? Differences of opinions prove that it all depends! It is interesting that two adages give the exact opposite advice, and really does depend upon to whom you are talking. If you are speaking to a group of cliff divers, you might remind them to "Look before you leap." Farmers may say, "He who hesitates is lost." There is some tension between these two ideals.

In the Bible there are also opposing concepts that have tension between them. It doesn't make either of them true; it simply means they're speaking to different situations. It is not too hard to overlook the tension between old adages, but it is not always so easy to overlook two different ideas when it is as fundamental as salvation.

The passage of scripture we are looking at today is the most controversial and misunderstood passage in the Book of James, and perhaps in the New Testament. One of the definitions of a cult, to the limitations of my knowledge, is that without exception they will try to use this text to prove that you have to work your way into heaven. Then, they add to the work. If you understand what I am talking about in this message, you will have an answer to those people who come to your door.

Jonathan H. Wilson

The Apostle Paul writes in Romans 8:28, "For we maintain that a man is justified by faith apart from observing the law." Paul says that we are made right with God by faith. It is a cornerstone of Christianity that if we are going to have a relationship with God it must be based on faith or trust in Him. Then, we read in James 2:24, "You see that a person is justified by what he does and not by faith alone." Paul says faith alone, or as Martin Luther wrote in the margin of his Bible, "Sole Fide" which means "faith alone." James comes along and says it is not just faith, but faith and works. They are talking about different things.

1. Who is correct—James or Paul?

a. Galatians 2:16, "...a man is not justified not by doing the law, but by faith in Jesus Christ." James 2:4, "It's not just faith, but faith and works. Over the years some people have said that what Paul wrote and what James wrote contradict one another and can't both be true. Reality is that they are both true, they were writing about two different things. Paul was fighting the problems of legalism.

b. Legalism...lazy faith. James was not fighting legalism, but the problem of lazy faith; those who say, "It doesn't matter what you do as long as you believe." They are fighting two different enemies. They are using the word "works" in two different ways.

c. Jewish laws...Christian lifestyle. When Paul uses "works," he is talking about Jewish laws—circumcision and things like that. When James uses the word "works," he is talking about the lifestyle of a Christian—acts of love. These are totally different.

d. Root of salvation...fruit of salvation. Paul focuses on the root of salvation, what happens to me internally? James focuses on the fruit of salvation...what happens on the outside. Jesus said, "By their fruits you will know them.

e. Know Christian...Show Christian. Paul is talking about how to know you are a Christian; James is talking about how to show you are a Christian. Paul is talking in his verse about how to become a believer on faith alone. Paul and James were asking two different questions, Paul was answering the question, "How do we receive salvation—and the final answer is not by works, but by faith. James seems to be asking the question, "How is faith recognized?" And, the final answer is...fruit! This is consistent with John the Baptist who said, "Every tree that does not bear fruit will be cut down." And of Jesus, who said, "I am the true vine. Every branch or Christian that does not bear fruit is taken away and cast forth into fire and burned." Jesus said, "By their fruit you will know them." James, Paul, and Jesus all say a version of the same thing. James is talking about how to behave like a believer. It is not a contradiction. Paul puts them all together in Ephesians 2:8-10, "...for it is by grace you have been saved, through faith, for a life of good works..." I have always said that good works are a response to, not a prerequisite for, salvation. Reality shows are hot right now on television. If you put the word "real" on something, it should sell more. "Real" leather, "real" coffee, "real" men don't eat quiche, etc. Coke was the "real" thing! James is defining what a real Christian is. He talks about the difference between real and counterfeit Christians; authentic believers and fake believers. James says there are five ways you can know you've got the real thing, that your faith is based on biblical reality.

2. What is reality faith?

a. Reality faith is not something you say. Verse 14, "What good is it, my brothers, if a man claims to have faith, but has no deeds? Can such faith save him?" Notice that he doesn't say he actually has faith; he just claims to have it. He talks about it. He knows all the right phases. There are a lot of people who claim to be Christians. George Gallop says that 50 million Americans say, "I'm born again" but you don't see anything in their lifestyle. Today, we tend to label people as Christians if they make the slightest sound of being a believer. It is more than just talk that is involved in real faith. Jesus said, "Not everyone who says to me 'Lord,' Lord is going to enter into the kingdom of heaven." Not everyone who professes to be a Christian is a possessor of Christianity. Larry Flint, the publisher of Hustler Magazine, said he was born again, but you never saw any changes in his life. He kept right on publishing pornography, no difference, and no change.

Jonathan H. Wilson

b. Reality faith is not something you feel. Verses 15-16, "Suppose one of your brothers is without clothes and daily food. If one of you says to him, 'Well goodbye, God bless you, stay warm and eat well,' but you don't give that person any food or clothing, what good does that do? I saw a Peanuts cartoon where Charlie Brown and Linus are inside, all cozy and warm, having a discussion on how sad it is that Snoopy is cold and hungry. "He's cold and hungry, we ought to do something about it." They walk out and say to Snoopy, "Be of good cheer, Snoopy." Do you know where Charles Schultz got that idea? From this verse... "What good is it?" Real faith is more than sympathy, feelings, and emotions. You act on it; you do something about it. It means getting involved.

c. Reality faith is not something you think. Verse 18, "Someone will say I have faith, I have deeds." For some people, faith is an intellectual trip, something to be studied, talked about, debated, and discussed. James is talking to those who have the mindset of "stimulate me intellectually, but don't ask me to get involved or make any kind of commitment." James says, "Show me your faith." Note the words "Show me..." If you claim to be a Christian, I have a right to ask you to prove it by looking at your lifestyle. Someone has said, "Faith is like calories. You can't see them, but you sure can see the results." I lived in two places in Missouri; the state theme is "The show me state." James would have made a good Missourian. You say you are a Christian? Prove it! Let me see the action that backs up your words. The children's choir has sung a chorus, "If you are saved and know it, then your life will really show it." Can you sing that song in good conscience? In his book, Why Not the Best, Jimmy Carter said that one of the turning points of his life was when somebody asked him, "If you were arrested for being a Christian, would there be enough evidence to convict you?" Know it—then show it!

d. Reality faith is something you believe. Verse 19, "You believe that there is one God, big deal, even the demons believe that... and shutter." The word "shutter" means "to bristle." When they hear about God, they bristle. James says that almost everyone believes in God. Big deal—everyone believes in God, even Satan, but that is not enough. George Barna, the poll researcher, "Many people believe, but don't practice." They said, "I'm a believer," but further questions said, the majority of those said they don't go to church,

The Good News About Hard Times

don't donate their time or their money. James would say that is a phony faith. Note also that we have been using the word "faith" and here is a subtle change of the word, from faith to belief. Faith and belief have the same root word. Let's look at the difference. Belief in our modern society has come to mean a certain acceptance of a set of ideas. Faith, on the other hand, involves an act of commitment that is not all present in the word "believe." James says believe all you want but that is not enough. Faith must involve action for it to be valid.

e. Reality faith is something you do. (Verses 20-25) James gives two very different examples—Abraham and Rahab. They were exact opposites. Abraham was a man, Rehab a woman. Abraham was a patriarch while Rahab was a prostitute. Abraham was somebody; Rahab was a nobody. In the Bible, Abe is a major character; Rahab was a minor character. James uses these characters to say it isn't important who you are as long as you have the important thing. They only had one thing in common. Their faith in God led them to action. Both had productive lives. You know the story of Abraham who proved his faith by offering to God his son Isaac on the altar. His faith was faith that resulted in action. Then he introduces Rahab. Rahab lived in Jericho where she sheltered spies sent to her by Joshua. It is one of the most striking stories of faith in the Bible. James was saying that the kind of faith those two had not been idle faith, but productive faith. They behaved in such a way that their belief came out visibly. The reality is "If you don't live it, you don't believe it!"

3. Reality success

a. Work – Faith = No success. You may have heard the story of a farmer who wanted to impress his hunting buddies. To impress them, he bought the smartest, most expensive hunting dog he could find. He trained this dog to do things no other dog on earth could do—impossible feats that would surely amaze anyone. Then, he invited the neighbors to go duck hunting with him. After a long, patient wait in the boat a group of ducks flew over and the hunters were able to make a few hits. Several ducks fell into the water. "Go get 'em!" shouted the proud owner to his magnificent dog. The dog leaped out of the boat, walked on the water, and picked up a bird and returned to the boat. As soon as he dropped the duck in the boat he trotted off across the water again and grabbed another

Jonathan H. Wilson

duck and brought it back to the boat. The owner beamed with pride as his wonderful dog walked across the water and retrieved each of the birds, one by one. Unable to resist the opportunity to brag a bit he asked his fellow hunters, "Do you notice anything unusual about my dog?" One of them rubbed his chin thoughtfully, "Yes," he finally said, "Come to think of it, I do. That silly dog doesn't know how to swim, does he?" Works without faith is not enough. Just as faith without works is not enough, works without faith is never good enough, either.

b. Faith − Works = No success. Have you heard the phrase, "Talk is cheap?" How about, "Actions speak louder than words"? Listen carefully, a cold, austere, intellectual faith; void of action is nothing more than a mental assent to the existence of God. It is just one step above atheism. It is long on words, but short in practice. James teaches us that this cold, intellectual type of faith is dead. It is the person who says he is a Christian but gives no evidence of it by what he does. This is the person who is in the church, but refuses to serve, give, or even attend unless it is convenient. Someone said, "Faith without works is like a screen door on a submarine—useless!" Faith without works is like having a headache and going and finding some Ibuprofen, believing that it will make me feel better, looking at the bottle, and putting it back on the shelf. Believing that it will make me better, but not putting that belief into action does me no good. That is James' point: What good is faith that is not put into action?

c. Faith + Works = Success. Two men were crossing the river in a rowboat when they got into an argument about faith and works. A third man, who was rowing turned to them and said, "I believe I can resolve this. In my hands I have two oars which I call faith and works. If I pull on one of them without the other, all we do is go around in circles. If I pull both of them simultaneously, we will move forward to our destination, using both of them at the same time." This is the way it is with faith and works. Faith without works will not suffice. Neither will works without faith. That is why in the final verse of this section James says that the people who intellectually assent to the doctrines of Christianity without practicing them is spiritually like a dead body. When physical death occurs, the soul is separated from

The Good News About Hard Times

the body. It begins to decay and compose. Our only hope is to repent, commit ourselves completely to Jesus Christ and begin to demonstrate our faith by our actions. Jesus tells us that our faith, our salvation, which is a free gift, should drive us to want to act as Christians. We should want to serve other people as well as our Lord. Time, you see, is a great taker. Once past, it is too late; it never returns. How it is used determines our satisfaction in life and our eternal destiny. A lot of people use their time only for themselves. They use their gifts only for themselves; use their resources only for themselves. Some live with the idea in their minds that says, "tomorrow I will help out so and so," but the problem is that tomorrow never comes. James says that faith that does not change the heart of an individual means nothing. A transformed heart wants to serve the kingdom of God. A genuine faith connection with God always causes the heart of a believer to want to serve, to do good deeds for Him. Why? Because they realize how fantastic it is to be saved by faith in Jesus. Because they want to share the gift that God gave them.

Well, I think that most people want to share the gift with others. Maybe I am naïve; maybe they don't want to share it. Maybe they just want to hoard it for themselves, perhaps because it is risky, that heaven forbid when we do something nice people might reject us. Yes, it is a risk.

Our call, as I see it, is to allow Christ to transform us from within and put our faith in action and to do what we can to save the world. I am a great admirer of Teddy Roosevelt. He was speaking in Chicago when he said, "Far better is it to dare mighty things, to win glorious triumphs even though checkered by failures, than to take rank with those poor spirits who neither enjoy nor suffer much because they live in a gray twilight of inactivity that knows not victory or defeat."

We are to find our spiritual gifts and get involved and use them. Some folks say, "Oh, I can't teach or be a Deacon or an Elder. That is okay. We are not all gifted in the same way, which is a good thing because we need multiple talents and abilities and gifts involved in this church in order to make it happen. Yes, we need Deacons and Elders but we also need people to do other things like help clean up our church grounds, paint over some old pealing spots. We need

Jonathan H. Wilson

Ushers, and other people to be involved at the church answering phones, etc. Every person in this room, with the exception of those who have only visited a few weeks, should be involved in some kind of ministry. It is putting the right personnel resource in the proper place. How do you do that?

Ed McManus says it this way, "You get some people together, and you leave them there for four hours. Then come back and find out how they are doing. If they don't look up when you come into the room, assign them to the Security Department. If they are counting the butts in the ashtray, put them in engineering. If they are screaming and waving their arms, send them off to manufacturing. And, if they've left early, put them in sales."

There is the story of the wealthy Rajah in India. He sent his son to a Western school. He wanted his son to have a part in all the activities, even including football. In his letter to the school he went on to say that he was going to send his servant to do the tackling, the blocking, and the running so that his son could have fun and the exercise but won't demean himself or risk himself. Significant action that contributes to life demands the risk of total involvement. Coming to faith in Christ is not the end but merely the beginning. I can always tell when somebody buys a new house in my neighborhood, even if I don't see him or her move in. You can see the results of new ownership.

Billy Graham once said, "There is no conflict between faith and works. In the Christian life faith and works go together like inhaling and exhaling. Faith is taking the gospel in; works is taking the gospel out."

When we do both when each person in the Body of Christ does their share of carrying the load, the weight of ministry becomes less. Remember the story that I told you about the man who was speaking. When the lights went out maintenance asked everyone to raise their hands, but only half of the hands went up. Again, "No, everyone put hands up!" Suddenly the lights went on and maintenance announced, "Many hands make light work."

The Good News About Hard Times

People throughout the history of this church have worked and sacrificed so that you and I could enjoy these facilities. Well, they are our responsibility now and we must keep them up for us and for the next generation. We need people to step forward and be willing to get involved. No more sending in the servants to do the blocking and tackling.

{"Tongue control must have been a serious problem because James talks about the tongue more than any other writer in the New Testament. One tenth of his letter is devoted to it"

Psalm 141:3 "Post a guard at my mouth God, Set a watch at the door of my lips"}

"The World's Biggest Trouble Maker/Encourager"

"Is Your Tongue Converted?"

Book of James - Chapter 10

James 3:1-12

Looking back, as we have been going through the Book of James, we see some characteristics of Christian maturity. We have seen that a mature Christian is patient in times of trouble. We have seen that a mature Christian is someone who behaves what they believe; practices their faith. This morning, we are to a third element and that is "control of our tongue." We have talked about the first two, so today we will focus on tongue control.

This must have been a serious problem because James talks about the tongue more than does any other writer in the New Testament. One-tenth of his letter is devoted to the subject. He refers to "tongue" 5 different times in 108 verses. It's obvious that the tongue and its use are absolutely essential and central to God's purpose in transforming people's lives. It is crucial. It is the litmus test of whether God is changing us or not. He is observing to see if we translated the truth of God's Word into our lifestyle.

In James 3, he is writing about two subjects. In Verses 1-12, he is talking about control of the tongue. In 3:13-18, he talks about wisdom. There is a close relationship between the tongue and wisdom. As a matter of fact, James 3 gives you two of the most telling tests for position of Christian leadership. If, for example, you want to nominate a person to a position of leadership in a church as an elder or deacon, or as a Sunday school teacher, there ought to be two questions to ask. (1) Can the person control his/her tongue? (2) Is the person wise, rational, and understanding? We will discuss wisdom further in the next two weeks.

1. The Importance of the Tongue

In those days, in the Israel culture, the rabbi was the top of the social, educational, and cultural totem pole. He was the person to whom everyone looked to with respect as a teacher. As the early

Jonathan H. Wilson

Christians were mostly from Jewish background, they understood the totem pole system and wanted, for the wrong reasons, to be on top of the pole. So, people started lining up to be teachers. In our culture, we have degenerated to the place where almost anyone can be a teacher. Nothing could be further from the biblical truth. James says, literally, "Not many of you should presume to be teachers, stop lining up to become teachers." James says, "Don't do that." In fact, he says the opposite, he says that nobody in their right mind should want to become a teacher. This is something for which you "...must be gifted and called." Why? Because teachers have a powerful influence on their students.

In my life, teachers have played a powerful role. I was a math-science major in high school. My calculus teacher in high school was brilliant, but knew nothing about motivating students. Because of his negative influence I withdrew my decision from going to college at Northup Institute of Technology to a lowly junior college because I didn't know what to do with my life if not an engineer. I then became a political science major, thinking about law school. Then, in my first year of college I ran into a law professor who sat at a desk and read from our law textbook. Boring! I dropped "poli-sci" as a major. Notice I am not giving names—until now!

Another college professor, Dr. Dina Stallings, motivated me in a beginning speech class and I thought I wanted to become a speech teacher. She required me to join the Debate Team. After six fruitless rounds of debate at a tournament at USC, where I would often agree with my opponent when they made a good case, Dr. Stallings kindly encouraged me to go into individual oratory. This I did with some success.

Another speech teacher, Dr. George Enell, who taught speech at Cal State Fullerton, encouraged me. He often invited me to bring a brown bag lunch to his office and talk about life, goals, and purpose. He was also an ordained pastor from Fuller Seminary and in one of those private discussions he suggested I think about seminary and the ministry, and we prayed together.

Another seminary professor, Dr. Bob Munger, got me interested in church renewal and church growth by first asking Patty and me to travel with him to share our testimony in several struggling,

The Good News About Hard Times

almost dying, churches. He then inspired me to turn-around patterns by sending me to churches that were growing. He would send me, claiming he didn't have time to go himself. He asked me to investigate the secret to growth, and to come back and teach his Church Growth class. I began to see common denominators in growing churches of all kinds and sizes. Dr. Munger also inspired me to come into the Presbyterian Church USA. Another teacher, Mr. Mel White, inspired me to focus on the communication of the gospel to the point of behavior or attitude change rather than on classical preaching. Another professor at Cal Grad School of Theology really got me interested in Biblical Ethics. I feel sure that every one of you could talk about the influence of some teacher or pastor that has had an impact in your life. Incidentally, good teachers are never paid enough. James was talking about the importance good teachers. What are the tools if a good teacher? Answer, "words!" Don't forget that. James then says, by the way, we all stumble in many ways. James makes it clear that every one of us sin. Sin is universal. We all sin.

The present continuous tense denotes repeated action. It occurs again and again. We have all sinned, we all are sinning, and we all will sin. And, if we say we have no sin, we are deceiving ourselves. James says so important is tongue control that if a person can control it completely he is a perfect man, for he has his whole body under control. He has reached the height of spiritual maturity. If you are looking for people with spiritual maturity, look for people who have tongue control. In the Bible, the height of spiritual knowledge is not how much Greek you know or Bible you know, but tongue control.

James goes on, "Friends, listen carefully. The last member of your body to be mastered is your tongue, and if you've got control of your tongue, you've got proof positive that the Holy Spirit has control of your life." Is James mistaken by connecting sins of the tongue with sins of the whole body? Not at all, because words usually lead to action. A person makes an unguarded remark in an unthinking moment and finds himself in a fight, sometimes verbal, sometimes even physical. James says his tongue slip has forced the rest of his body to defend itself. Now, in order to impress upon us the importance of controlled speech and the consequences of our words, James gives us three distinct powers of the tongue and six illustrations of the tongue.

2. The power of the tongue

a. Power to direct. (Verses 1-4) Bit and rudder. Compared are the horse and the bit. As an Air Force kid, my family moved around. I was born in Buffalo, New York, then went to Florida, then to Missouri. I was a city kid, never had I been near a horse. We lived on a farm near where my stepdad commanded a small Air Force base and I helped out Mr. Collip on the farm. Driving a stick shift truck and a tractor on a farm at ten years old was no big deal back then in the Midwest. We had acres of alfalfa, lots of chickens, and hundreds of black heifer cows—but no horses. I was ten years old and the nearest neighbors were the Curtis family. They had three kids, Jimmy, Tommy, and Karen, my first girlfriend, though she probably never knew it. They all rode their horses over to our farm one summer day. They asked me if I'd like to ride and I said, "Sure," thinking I'd really impress Karen. After all, I'd grown up listening on the radio (no television) to "The Lone Ranger." "Hi, ho, Silver, away!" Remember? The Curtis kids kind of grinned at each other as some of you who know horses can imagine. I put my foot in the stirrup and grabbed the horn with both hands and started to pull myself up, ready to say, "Hi, ho Silver, away!" Well, as those of you who know horses already know, the horse took off like a shot and galloped at full speed across a pasture until it stopped at a female horse. Years later, I began to understand that. Here I was hanging on to the horn for dear life, while my feet went up under the horse. I was hoping and praying the saddle would not slide off the horse. What I didn't know was about this little thing called a bit that goes in the mouth of a horse that keeps it under control. I didn't impress Karen too much. However, her brother Jimmy taught me later that day that the reigns are more than just a leather strap to hold a horse, but they are reigns with a bit at the end with which a ten-year-old boy can control a 1,000-pound animal.

Next, James talks about a ship and a rudder. The captain of the ship determines the direction of a ship by a small rudder. If you have ever seen a ship in dry-dock you know how small a rudder is in comparison to the huge ship. In selecting the bit and rudder, James selected two items that are small in themselves, yet exercise great power. A small bit enables a rider to control a huge horse; a small rudder enables a pilot to steer a great ship. Both the bit and the rudder must overcome contrary forces. James writes: "A bit in the mouth of a horse controls the whole horse. A small rudder on a huge ship in the hands of a skilled captain sets a course in the strongest of winds. A word out of your mouth may seem of no account, but it can accomplish nearly anything, or destroy it." The bit must overcome the wild nature of the horse. The rudder must overcome the wild winds and storms of nature that would drive the ship off course. We, too, have a contrary force that makes us want to get off course. There are circumstances that make us say things that we ought not to say. Sin on the inside and pressures on the outside are seeking control of the tongue. The bit and the rudder when misused affect many lives. Did any of you see USA's front-page story about the most dangerous occupation in America? The number one most dangerous occupation was that of the fisherman, those who fish for a living. More people die from fishing accidents than any other occupation. Why? The biggest cause was pilot error. Most of the time the person in charge guided the rudder in the wrong direction during turbulent times. A runaway horse, a misguided ship, and an unrestrained tongue often injure those we love. The words we speak affect the lives of others. No wonder David prayed: "Post a guard at my mouth, God, set a watch at the door of my lips." (Psalm 141:3)

b. Power to destroy. (Verse 5-8) Fire and animals. Next James says, "The tongue is a fire, a world of evil among the parts of the body. It corrupts the whole person; it sets the whole course of his life on fire. The smallest spark wipes out the most delightful forest." Listen to Peterson in "The Message" on this verse: "It only takes a spark, remember, to set off a forest fire. A careless or wrongly placed word out of your mouth can do that. By our speech we can ruin the world, turn harmony to chaos, throw mud onto a reputation, send the whole world up in smoke and go up in smoke with it, smoke right from the pits of hell."

We used to vacation every summer at Pine Mountain Lake near Yosemite, I think one of the most beautiful lakes in the Western United States. We were playing golf on the high mountain golf course when this vicious storm came up. Within a few minutes we could see lightning strikes off in the distance. As we went back to our cabin near the lake, we saw smoke. A terrible fire had broken out near Yosemite. We were planning on going into Yosemite the next day but the road was closed, as the smoke was everywhere even though it was 20 miles away. In a couple of days, smoke was so thick we could hardly breathe. One day we couldn't even see the sky. We were never able to go into the area. The next year when we drove into the area, we could not believe the devastation. Thousands of acres of timber, beautiful pines, and redwoods had gone up in smoke and forever scared by the destruction from a single fire. Like a fire, the tongue can heat things up quickly. If you put a controlling person or the clinical term, a person with a "borderline personality disorder" coupled with a hot temper and unrestrained tongue you have a firestorm, whether it is in a home, business, or church. David wrote in Psalm 39:1, "I'm determined to watch steps and tongue so they won't land me in trouble. I decided to hold my tongue as long as the wicked is in the room. 'Mum's the word,' I said and kept quiet, but the longer I kept silent the worse it got. My insides got hotter and hotter. My thoughts boiled over; I spilled my guts." A hot head and a hot heart can lead to burning words. Like a fire, an uncontrolled tongue can heat things up. Proverbs 18:21, "Words kill, words give life; they're either poison or fruit. You choose." Don't believe it? Listen to this, someone has calculated that for every word in Hitler's Mein Kampf, 125 lives were lost in World War II. That is the destructive nature of the tongue. On the other hand, there is a good part of the fire because most of us would not be here this morning if we didn't have a car with a little fire in the engine. Fire, but note that it is always fire under control that will cook most of what we eat for dinner tonight. The tongue is a tremendous gift given to us by God. The question is, is it under control?

Next, James says, "The tongue is also like a wild animal. It is restless and cannot be ruled and it seeks its prey and pounces and kills." Do you remember "Lion Country Safari" down where the 405 and the 5 freeways meet? You could drive through while animals wandered around in the native habitat. We used to take our boys there. The animals didn't look dangerous, but signs were posted, "Do Not Under Any Circumstances Leave Your Car." "Do Not Open Your Windows" which meant you would be some lion's lunch. Well, Lion Country Safari is long gone. Freeways have paved over much of it, but the other reason is the number of people who were duped by the tame look of the wild animals, and got out of their cars and were mauled,

The Good News About Hard Times

injured or worse. Wild animals may look tame, but don't turn your back on them—just as the tongue has the power to destroy. If people cannot control their tongue, the minute your back is turned they will rip into you.

c. Power to delight. (Verses 9-11) Fountain and trees. The drinking fountain, of course, provides the cool, refreshing water that a man needs to stay alive. In Romans 15:32, Paul prayed that the Roman Christians would refresh the hearts of the saints. Paul often referred to believers as those who "refreshed him." Yes, the tongue can be used for good, but that was not James' concern. If that were the issue, the letter would not have been written. Those who control their tongues don't need an urgent letter. What James was concerned about was the inconsistency of the tongue of some believers. James says, "With our tongues we bless God our father; with the same tongues we curse the very men and women he made in his image. Curses and blessings out of the same mouth! My friends this can't go on. A spring doesn't gush fresh water one day and brackish the next, does it? Apple trees don't bear strawberries, do they? Raspberry bushes don't bear apples, do they? You're not going to dip into a polluted mud hole and get a cup of clear, cool water, are you?" No one should feel ignored. Remember that James said in Verse 2, "We all stumble." We all do it. Sin is inclusive! Some people in some churches go to church and sing something we don't sing anymore, "Take my lips and let them be, consecrated Lord to thee." They then leave and go into the fellowship hall for coffee and instead of ministering to people and seeking to be a blessing to the dozens of hurting people all around us, their tongues begin the Sunday worship critique. It is open season—the choir number was too fast or too slow. The song leader was too frisky; the Scripture reading was too long; the reader was not prepared and didn't read the right translation. The lights are too dim. The ushers were too unfriendly or someone else was too friendly; the amount in the offering plate was too small; the parking was a mess; that preacher was aiming right at me. He must have been listening into our conversations. He was too long, too psychological, too theological, too practical, too extemporaneous, too many stories, not enough stories, too personal, not personal enough. We've all heard them all! Instead of applying the message of the Bible and worship service, they critique the messengers. Let me apologize to everyone here today. You have to understand I am

Jonathan H. Wilson

not talking about any of you, but boy, that crowd last Sunday, wow! They were really something! They saw the sermon text and didn't even want to come today. James was pointing out the problem of the inconsistent tongue. He makes the point that you never find that in nature. Good water and bad water do not come out of the same fountain. A fig tree doesn't bear olives. A grapevine doesn't bear figs. Inconsistency is a problem. Take the water fountain at the entrance of the sanctuary or the one between the classrooms and the Fellowship Hall. Sometimes the water is good if you let it run long enough, sometimes bad. But, people usually drink it only once. You don't gamble. You only drink water that is consistent. Don't worry, we are forming a committee soon that will address these and other issues like it, prioritizing them with other things to get this campus in shape and with little money. Hopefully, instead of one person working on these problems, we are going to have a committee. Soon the water will be refreshing and consistent or it will be a flowerbed. Until then, I myself would not trust it. By the way, the coffee and punch are outstanding! The church is making a lot of progress. Yesterday, we had 30 to 40 people all over this campus—in the rain—cleaning out closets of 40 years of "stuff." We had a huge cherry picker in this room changing bulbs high up in the sanctuary so you can see better this morning. Even the power-point light bulb was replaced. Many are to be commended from both the English group and the Spanish-speaking group. I don't want to single any one person out because there were many here, not all at one time, and I couldn't mention them all. However, I was really excited by the turnout and the progress, much of which cannot be seen unless you open a hundred closets and know what was in them before. That is a side issue, but the church needs to be consistent. If a visitor drinks from a bad fountain they may wonder what else is wrong.

Back to James' point, James is saying, "Nature is always consistent." No squirrel ever gets up in the morning and says, "I'm tired of this rat race. I'm not going out to collect nuts any more; that's a nutty idea. From now on I'm into Krispie Kremes." Neither do birds go on strike and say, "I'm not going to sing or chirp anymore. I'm going to join the choir." No, they just continue to do that for which they were created. James says, "Nature is consistent," but here is the scary part: No man can tame the tongue. Jesus says, "Out of the abundance of a man's heart, the

The Good News About Hard Times

mouth speaks." In Paul's list of the fruit of the spirit, self-control is one of the "Fruit of the Spirits" that resides in us. When James says, "No man" can control the tongue, he is also saying it is only the Holy Spirit that can control the tongue. Only when the Lord is transforming our hearts, will what comes out of our mouths be under His control. By the way, so that you will not forget, during the offering the ushers will be passing out a business card I had made up yesterday at the printer. They will pass this card out and I want you to take these cards home and tape it to the mirror where you wash your face, brush your teeth, and sharpen your tongue; and, memorize the two verses. One verse out of Proverbs and the other is when David prays a wonderful prayer in Psalm 141:3. It is one of my favorite Bible prayers. "Post a guard at my mouth, God, set a watch at the door of my lips." Read those words, pray them and ask the Holy Spirit to help you live them because you can't control your tongue on your own power.

3. Results of tongue control

a. Consistency. When you control your tongue, people like to be around you because they know you will be consistent. Paul prayed for the Romans to be refreshing to each other. Don't you love that visual? Isn't that great? Wouldn't you like to be known as an encourager, someone who is refreshing to be around? We should start calling the Fellowship Hall the "Refreshment Hall," not because of the food, but because of the refreshment we get from being around loving, caring people.

b. Trust. When you have tongue control on a consistent basis, people learn to trust you.

c. Leadership. Nobody likes a "hot head" that loses his or her cool to be in control. Leaders tend to get their point across without losing their cool.

4. Positive tongue control

a. The grace of appreciation. Have you learned the therapy of thanksgiving? We spend too much of our time sitting around sucking our thumbs and asking "Why me Lord? Here I am trying to be good, read my Bible, love you, and am kind to people...and this is what I get. This burden?" I remember one guy who walked

Jonathan H. Wilson

into my counseling office about 20 years ago and I mean he "unloaded the truck" about his wife. He began, "You won't believe the woman I'm married to." I said, "Tell me about her," and he did at lengths—gusts up to 90 miles per hour—for about 45 minutes. He ran her into the ground for the whole time, and then came up for air. I said, "You mean you married a woman like that?" He said, "She wasn't that way when I married her." Being very tactful, I said, "You mean you made her that way?" I asked him to go home and do an assignment and not to come back until it was done. I asked him to write down on a piece of paper all the things that he appreciated about this woman. About a week later, he came back smiling. He says, "I've decided to keep her!" "Oh really, how come?" He had decided that if he had a woman that good he'd better keep her. He later became a Christian, got into a Bible study, and several years later became an elder in our church. He has now served three terms as an elder in that church; still married to the same woman. Throughout my years in ministry, I have found that most relationships are destroyed by people focusing on the negative, rather than on the positive. Critics of the coming pre-school say we might need one of those rooms; we might be inconvenienced; we might have to clean out the closets fix the drinking fountains; fix the air-conditioning and heating system; and improve the playground. The positive is that 60 children and their families will be exposed to the ministry of this church, an opportunity to start building once again with young families; and, over the life of the contract, $200,000 at $5,000 per month. Let's focus on the positive, not the negative.

By the mid-2nd Century, one Christian wrote, "We are everywhere. We are in your towns and in your cities, we are in your army and navy; we are in your palaces; we are in the senate, we are more numerous than anyone." By 300 AD, the church was spreading so fast that it appeared the entire civilized world could be evangelized by the year 500 AD. But, an unthinking Augustine decreed at the Counsel of Nicea in 305 AD that "Everyone in the empire was already Christian." Suddenly, there was no need for missionaries. Stop the sending! Put the ship in the harbor. Slowly, ever so slowly, a deadly perversion of the Gospel began to prevail. A division in the church developed between clergy and laity. No longer was every Christian considered a capable minister or missionary. Slowly the idea prevailed that only trained clergy were truly qualified to

The Good News About Hard Times

minister or share the Gospel. As a result, the Christian movement, after spreading like fire, slowed to a crawl. Friends, only when we get back to the idea that we are all called to ministry, not to critique each other, will the church get back to what it was called to do! Therefore, every one of you are called to find a place to use your gifts and talents and get involved in ministry.

I wrote these words very early this morning so they are not complete, but here is a summary of what is ministry today?:

- Ministry is being patient in times of trouble because you know that the Lord is holding your hand.

- Ministry is behaving like you say you believe, so that others will know you are a Christian by your love.

- Ministry is going out in the rain to clean closets that most people will never notice, much less ever appreciate, but you do it as unto the Lord.

- Ministry is going to church to minister to and to hear God s Word, even if you would like to stay warm by a fire.

- Ministry is having faith in others, even when they let you down time and time again.

- Ministry is spending hours to prepare to teach a lesson that few really want to hear, except the Lord.

- Ministry is caring for others, not because you will gain anything of benefit, but because He cares for you and they need your care.

- Ministry is giving things to the poor, not because you have worn them out, but because someone else could wear them and you don t.

- Ministry is controlling your tongue until you have asked God to put a guard over your mouth.

- Ministry is being thoughtful of people of another culture because God made them, too, and God has blessed you.

Jonathan H. Wilson

- Ministry is speaking words of life to another when you need them yourself.

- Ministry is using your tongue to build and delight, instead of to tear down and destroy.

- Ministry is giving someone fruit, or a Krispie Kreme, someone to whom you haven't always been nice.

- Ministry is being an encourager, even when you need encouragement.

- Ministry is affirming someone when you feel the need for affirmation.

- Ministry is showing appreciation to someone when you need to be appreciated.

- Ministry is to give, even when you feel like keeping and receiving.

- Ministry is praying for someone else when you feel the need yourself for prayer.

- Ministry is taking the time to feed others when your own soul is hungry.

- Ministry is telling the truth to people even when you can't see the results.

- Ministry is hurting with other people even when your own hurts can't be shared.

- Ministry is keeping your word even when it would be easier to break a promise.

- Ministry is being faithful to commitments even when the flesh wants to run away.

- Ministry is making someone else feel worthwhile even when you feel worthless.

The Good News About Hard Times

••••   Ministry is forgiving others even when they don t think they need it.

Remember, my people, WORDS KILL, WORDS GIVE LIFE; THEY'RE EITHER POISON OR FRUIT—YOU CHOOSE. Words of life, fruit, the evidence that the Holy Spirit is truly transforming your life.

Pray this prayer this week, as David did, "Post a guard at my mouth, God, set a watch at the door of my lips."

{"While clinging to the symbols of affluence they froze to death; the worlds false values and false wisdom cost them their very lives."

James 1:5 "If any of you lacks wisdom, he should ask God who gives wisdom generously"}

"How to Relate Wisely to People"

"Wisdom from the Kingdom of Light"

Book of James - Chapter 11

James 3:13-18

In 1845, a Royal Navy Rear Admiral, Sr. John Franklin and 128 officers and men left England to find what has become known as the Northwest Passage. They sailed in two three-mast ships. Each ship was equipped with an auxiliary system engine and a 12-day supply of coal in case steam power would be needed somewhere along the anticipated two- to three-year journey. They could have taken a lot more, but instead of loading additional coal, each ship made room for a 1,200-volume library and luxuries such as an organ and full elegant place setting for all china, cut glass goblets, and sterling flatware. The officer's sterling was engraved with the officer's family crests and initials on the heavy handles. The Franklin Expedition was patterned after the extravagant officers' clubs in England. The only clothing these proud Englishmen took were their uniforms and greatcoats of Her Majesty's navy. The two ships sailed off with great pomp and glory. Two months later a British whaler met the two ships in the Lancaster Sound and reports were carried back to England of the expedition's high spirits. He was the last to see them alive. Search parties, funded by Lady Jane Franklin, began to piece together a tragic history from information gathered from Eskimos. Some had seen men pushing a boat across a lake, the remains of 30 men were found in a tent in Terror Bay. Three wooden masts were found protruding through the ice in Simpson Strait. For the next 20 years search parties recovered skeletons from the frozen waste. Twelve years later it was found that Rear Admiral Franklin had died on board the ship. The remaining officers and crew had decided to walk for help. They found a clump of bodies; with the bodies they found place settings of sterling silver flatware bearing the officer's initials and family crests. The officer's remains were still dressed in their fine, buttoned uniforms; many with silk scarves still in place. The expedition itself accomplished absolutely nothing. Yet, it is universally agreed that it was the turning point in Arctic exploration. The mystery of the expedition's disappearance and its fate attracted so much attention in Europe and in the United States that no less than 30 ships made extended journeys in search of an answer. In so doing they mapped the Arctic for the first time, discovered the Northwest Passage, and developed a technology suitable for the Arctic climate. It was upon the shipwreck of Admiral Franklin's "wisdom" that Adundsen would one day stand victorious at the South Pole and the Hensen brothers at the North.

Now, listen carefully, it is in a similar way that the shipwreck of the wisdom of the Kingdom of Darkness ought to motivate us to seek wisdom from above, wisdom from the Kingdom of Light, so that we can navigate wisely through life. This is what James is getting at when he contrasted two kinds of wisdom in Verses 13-18. In Verse 13-16 he shows us the skeletons of earthly wisdom. Such earthly wisdom does not come down from heaven but is earthly, unspiritual, and of Satan.

In Verses 15-16, he shares the result of earthly wisdom "for where you find envy and selfish ambition, there you will find disorder and every evil practice. In contrast, James shows the incredible difference of heavenly wisdom and describes seven beautiful characteristics of heavenly wisdom in particular regard to relationships with people.

All day long, every day of the year, we encounter people. Some people are a delight to be around, some are very difficult. Others are inspiring people you touch and you go away inspired. Other people are irritating, fascinating, and some attempt to be intimidating. The fact is that a lot of the problems we have in life are because of personality conflicts. We don't get along with people. When your relationships are bad, life is miserable. It is very important that we learn how to get along with people. James gives us some practical advice.

Verse 18 is the climax of this section, "...and those who are peacemakers will plant seeds of peace and reap a harvest of goodness." James is saying that every day, in every relationship, we are planting seeds. Seeds of anger, jealousy, peace, confidence, insecurity, and many different kinds of seeds. So, James says that you will reap the kind of relationship you sow.

Wisdom helps us be wise in the kind of relationships we plant because it is out of that growth that will come our future relationships with that person. A lot of times we treat people in foolish ways or

The Good News About Hard Times

self-serving ways and we provoke the exact opposite behavior that we would normally like to see. By the way, common sense is not really so common. A lot of smart people are not so wise. They may be educated but they're a washout in relationships.

James, in this passage, does three things:

He defines real wisdom.

He shows how it is different from human wisdom.

He shows how it operates.

Assumptions about wisdom

Wisdom is a lifestyle. (Verse 13) James states clearly that wisdom has nothing to do with your intelligence. It has everything to do with your relationships and your character. James asks if we want to be counted wise, to build a reputation for wisdom? Here is what we need to do: Live well, live wisely, and live humbly. It is the way you live, not the way you talk that counts.

Suppose that James were preaching here this Sunday and asking, "Let me see the hands of those that are wise?" If you were dumb enough to raise your hand, he would say, "Prove it! Show me! Show me your wisdom by your lifestyle."

In Verse 13, "Boasting that you are wise isn't wisdom. It's not a matter of what you say with your lips, but a matter of what you live with your life. Not a matter of words, but of works." Wisdom is not so much a matter of diplomas on the walls, but an attitude that shows how wise you really are. How do you get along with other people? That shows how wise you really are. It's a lifestyle! Wisdom has more to do with character in relationships than it has to do with education and intelligence. Wisdom creates humility. Knowledge causes pride, but wisdom causes humility. Wisdom is applying the knowledge you have to everyday life in building better and stronger relationships. It is not knowing facts; you can know facts and never apply them. James said, "Be doers of the word, not hearers only." You can know right from wrong. That is knowledge. Wisdom is applying that knowledge to your life to make a positive impact on how you live your life in a proper relationship with others.

Lack of wisdom causes problems. (Verse 14-16) "Mean spirited ambition isn't wisdom. Twisting the truth to make yourself sound wise isn't wisdom. It's the furthest thing from wisdom; it's animal cunning, devilish conniving." James says that whenever you're trying to look better than others or get the better of others, it is not of God, "... things fall apart and everyone ends up at the other's throats." Lack of wisdom causes all kinds of disorder, problems, chaos and confusion in our lives. When you see someone that is unstable, unreliable, hopping from church to church, causing confusion and disorder in the church, you will know that that person is not operating or living their life with Godly wisdom. They don't know where they belong or where they fit in. The Bible says that such people are driven and motivated by bitter and envious feelings and selfish feelings. James is saying, "Stop living your life with ungodly and worldly wisdom from the Kingdom of Darkness. Start living with wisdom from the Kingdom of Light. Allow God to teach you through the Holy Spirit, how to apply the truth of His word to your life. How can I know if I am wise in how I relate with people? Today we're going to take a wisdom test to see how wise you really are. James, in Verse 17, lists characteristics of wise people.

How to relate wisely to people

Wise people have integrity. "Real wisdom, God's wisdom, begins with a holy life." Holy means uncorrupted, authentic. In 1 John 3:3 this word refers to Christ's character. Integrity—If I'm wise, I'm not going to lie to you, I'm not going to cheat you, I'm not going to manipulate you, I'm not going to be deceitful. I'll be a person of integrity because all relationships are built on trust and respect. If you don't have honesty, who is going to trust you? If you don't have trust, who is going to respect you? You have to have integrity in your life. There are two books in the Bible that talk a lot about wisdom, James in the New Testament and Proverbs in the Old Testament. Proverbs 10:9 says, "The man of integrity walks securely." He is not afraid of being found out, because he doesn't say one thing to one group and another thing to another group. A great and respected senator some years ago said, and forgive me if I forgot who it was, maybe someone can tell me, and reporters once asked him, "How do you remember what you said to this group and to that group, so as to not get tripped up? He said, "Simple, I don't have a good enough memory to be a habitual liar, so I just tell the truth." Eventually, you are going to slip up. If you have integrity, you have confidence then

The Good News About Hard Times

you walk securely in your relationships. You know you're not putting people on.

Wise people work at maintaining harmony "...is characterized by getting along with others." Wise people work at maintaining harmony. They are not always looking for a fight. Did you ever meet someone who is always arguing, always looking for a fight? Did you hear about the man who was so argumentative he would only eat food that disagreed with him? Proverbs 20:3 says, "Any fool can start arguments. The wise thing is to stay out of them." Three things that James says cause arguments, if you are wise you will avoid them:

a. Comparing – "You're just like...", "Why can't you be more like..." "My first husband..." 2 Corinthians 10:12 says, "It is unwise to compare."

b. Condemning – "It's all your fault, you should be ashamed," "You always, you never, you ought to, you should, you shouldn't." Someone has said, "You can bury a relationship with a lot of little digs."

c. Contradicting – How do you like to be interrupted in the middle of a sentence? It is irritating. James says that if you are wise you don't sweat the small stuff. Another James, William James, said the secret of wisdom is knowing what to overlook. Some things are just not worth the fight. Proverbs 14:29, "A wise man controls his temper. He knows that anger causes mistakes." Have any of you done something in anger that you later regretted? Anger causes mistakes.

3. Wise people are gentle and reasonable. "...is gentle and reasonable." A wise person can learn from anyone. Literally it says, "Wisdom is submission." This word is used only one time in the New Testament. It doesn't really mean submissive. It means reasonable, willing to listen, willing to be open to new ideas. The Revised Standard Version says, "Open to reason." The Living Bible says, "it allows discussion." Are you a reasonable person? Can your kids reason with you? The Bible says, "If you're wise you are reasonable." You're open to suggestions. Do you know anyone who has the attitude: "Don't confuse me with the facts, I've made up my mind"? James says that's stupid. A wise person can learn from anyone.

Jonathan H. Wilson

A new pastor preaches his first sermon. When it is over a guy greets the new pastor at the door: "Pastor, that sermon stunk." The pastor is hurt but trying to be real open and wise about it, "What did you not like about it?" "In the first place, you read it. In the second place, you read it poorly. Third, it wasn't worth reading in the first place." Another guy walks out right behind him and says, "Don't listen to old Jim. He just repeats what he hears everybody else say." "Gentle" is also translated, "considerate" which means being mindful of the feelings of others. There is a common mistake that if I don't feel the way you feel, then your feelings must be invalid or illogical or irrational or silly. James says that wise people are considerate; they don't minimize the feelings of other people. Proverbs 15:4, "Kind words bring life, but cruel words crush your spirit." Often times when we react to people's emotions we say things that hurt. Often we belittle their feelings. We put them down. James says if we are wise, we will be considerate of the feelings of others.

Did you ever play the game, "My dad can beat your dad"? Husband comes home worn out and complaining, "The traffic was terrible on the 101. An accident piled up traffic for miles. My boss is mad at me, the air-conditioning went out at the office, and the toilet backed up." The wife says, "Oh you think you had a hard day. I not only had a hard day at work but when I came home the microwave died, the vacuum broke, and junior flushed the cat down the toilet, just before I had to rush him to Emergency for a broken arm." The fact is that they both had a bad day. Wisdom is consideration for the other person. They've both had a bad day.

4. Wise people overflow with mercy. "...overflowing with mercy and blessing." Do you jump on people every time they blunder? Every time they make a mistake and fumble the ball? That's dumb! Wisdom is full of mercy. Do you ever let people go, or do you gunnysack their past mistakes and sins? Do you hold them in leverage and never let them go free even if they ask for forgiveness? "Remember when you did such and such?" You're always holding on and bringing up the past for leverage. That is unfair and James would say it is dumb. If you're wise, you won't bring up past mistakes. Instead, you will be full of mercy. We should give what is needed, not what is deserved, just as our Lord died on the cross to give us what we need not what we deserve.

The Good News About Hard Times

Two guys were at a convention with their wives. They were long lost friends. They sat in the lobby all night talking. They knew they would be in trouble with their wives when they went back to their rooms. The next day they happened to see each other, "What did your wife think?" "I walked in the door and my wife got historical." "Don't you mean hysterical?" "No, historical—she told me everything I ever did wrong." Wise people don't emphasize our past mistakes. Proverbs 17:9, "Love forgets mistakes. Nagging about them parts even the best of friends." If you are wise you won't rub it in; you will rub it out." You won't hold it over their heads—you forget it! When somebody stumbles, you don't pull out all the ammunition and blast them; you don't judge them, you encourage them. Friends, we don't need judgment. We need encouragement when we stumble. Are you that way? If someone does something you don't like, if someone forgets to put gas in the tank and you run out of gas on the freeway, how do you react? What do you do in response? In my home as a youngster, every mistake was a capital offense and to be honest with you I couldn't wait to get out on my own. After Patty and I were married we soon learned that the patterns of our families of origin were not going to work. The terms that we have tried to use in our house when someone makes a mistake is "Those things happen." If someone drops a glass and breaks it, "Those things happen." Most people know when they have done something wrong. If not, they may repeat it over and over again in which case it needs to be recognized as a mistake, but then forgiven—not rubbed in, but rubbed out. The wise person will not emphasize the mistake. James says, "Wisdom is full of mercy and 'good fruit.'" The word for good fruit is also translated "blessing," but the old down-to-earth term is "kindness." "Good fruit" is kindness in action; it is something you do. It is not just showing sympathy. You don't just say, "I feel for you." If possible, you do something about it. You take action. It is a kindness; it is being a doer of the Word.

5. Wise people are consistent. "...not hot one day and cold the next." James is saying, "You want to be wise, be consistent." He has talked about that before when he talked about the water fountain in Verse 1l, "...good like water." Wise people are consistent, reliable, predictable." Leaders are always selected from a pool of consistent leaders. Can you imagine the President in Chief or the Commander of the Allied Forces, Tommy Franks, or any of the leaders in this war being "hotheads"? Unpredictable? Hotheads never make it through

the first weeks of Basic Training. They would "wash out" of basic training; you can't have a person who is "hot" one day and "cold" the next, always running on their emotions when in charge of anything or in dealing with people. Wise people are always under control.

Wise people are not phony. "...not two-faced." The mark of a wise person is that they are not hypocritical. In the Greek theatre they would often have two or three actors playing several parts. They would just hold different masks in front of their faces. One actor would have five or six parts and that actor was described as a hypocrite. That is the same word that is used here. It means "without hypocrisy." James says if you are wise you will not try to be something you are not. I've said this before, if you think you are perfect, this is the wrong church for you. And by the way, if you have to have a perfect pastor, you might as well find another church right now. If you insist on wearing a mask, this isn't the church for you. This church is for real people with real sins, with real hang-ups, with real faults, real emotional problems, and real family problems. Real people are honest and open. They're not phony. They're genuine. They're real and authentic. "What you see is what you get with a wise person. They don't attain to or pretend perfection. James says that if you are wise you're not going to disguise your weakness. Of course, you have to be somewhat discerning, but there are so many phony relationships today with people who are trying to be what they are not. The number one place for this is in singles bars. Phony relationship—where else in society do you offer to buy something for a total stranger? Phony! These people are trying to be something they are not. Another place is the Internet. People are being duped all the time by people they meet on the Internet. People say all kinds of things they are not. Reality TV shows also promote it. Pretend you are a millionaire on national television for 15 weeks and people eat it up; the ratings for these shows go through the roof. Why? I wonder if it isn't because everyone has been duped and it's kind of fun to see someone else duped. Misery loves company. Then, when the truth is revealed, all these girls dump the guy, even the one with the huge engagement ring. Why? It may be because he doesn't have a million, but I personally don't think so. In reality, I think most of the time it is because these women realize that this guy was, for all this time, trying to be someone he wasn't. Proverbs 28:13, "You will never succeed in life if you try to hide your sins." I don't mean that you don't use some discretion. You dump the whole manure wagon

The Good News About Hard Times

on someone on the first date and you probably will never see him or her again. But then again, maybe that would eliminate these "fall in love at first look" relationships. You'd never get past the first round on Elimi-Date. James says that it is dumb to try to pretend that you are perfect, that you've got it all together because nobody else does. So, they are just going to put you under a microscope and wait until they see a flaw and say, "Ah-hah!" When you start telling other people your weaknesses, you may be surprised to find out that they are not shocked, because they already knew. Everybody knows your weaknesses. We see each other's weaknesses all the time. Why do we walk around pretending that we don't have any? We do. It is so obvious to everybody. Wise people are not stupid, but they are also not phony.

7. A church of wise people is healthy. "You can develop a healthy, robust community that lives right with God and enjoy its results only if you do the hard work of getting along with each other, treating each other with dignity and honor." James says that wise people, acting wisely in a church community, will be a peaceful church and reap a harvest of goodness. James is here reaching for a fitting climax to this section about earthly wisdom. He is saying in summary that the Lord wants us to reject the decaying skeletons of earthly wisdom, of the Kingdom of Darkness. Such wisdom he says does not come down from heaven, but from the minds of men influenced by Satan. For where you find envy and selfish ambition, there you find every disorder and evey evil practice. Listen carefully, in the Kingdom of Darkness the bones and grinning skulls of such false wisdom are clumped everywhere along the shore. Among them are the remains of many churches freezing to death. While clinging to the symbols of affluence, they froze to death; the world's false value and false wisdom cost them their very lives. We need to be like the ships that followed Franklin's Expedition, learning from his costly mistakes, enlightened from the folly of the world's wisdom, and embracing the new wisdom from the Kingdom of Light. Friends, we must consciously take hold of the wisdom from heaven and the Kingdom of the Light. Again, a good point to remember is the promise given earlier in James' letter: "If any of you lacks wisdom, he should ask God who gives (wisdom) generously." (James 1:5)

{12. "Why do people rob banks, kill each other, spouses abuse each other, children kill each other over a pair of shoes. Why do we hurt those we love? Not all, but much of the time we hurt people because we envy them"

James 4:2 "You want what you don't have, you long for what others have"}

"A subject that we don't like to talk about"

"Why Do We Hurt the Ones We Love?"

Book of James - Chapter 12

James 4:1-10

Our world is in a crisis. The news seems so tense everywhere that I thought I'd begin with some true news stories that are not so serious in nature but that make the point of today's message.

The Ann Arbor News crime column reported that a man walked into a Burger King in a small town in Michigan, at 7:50 a.m., flashed a gun and demanded cash. The quick thinking clerk turned him down because he said he couldn't open the cash register without a food order. When the man ordered onion rings, the clerk said they weren't available for breakfast. The man, totally frustrated, walked away.

A 20-year-old woman Karen Lee Joachimmi, was arrested in small town in Florida, for attempted robbery of a Howard Johnson's motel. She was armed with only an electric chain saw, which however was not plugged in.

Three young men decided, late one night, to hold up a gas station. Taking baseball bats and knives they entered and demanded money from the station clerk. The clerk was an ex-Israeli Army officer and unarmed combat instructor. Needless to say, the three men ended up in the hospital, for a long time. (The station owner pressed no charges.)

A frustrated woman in Germany decided that Oil of Olay was no longer turning the trick for her, so she decided that she would bathe in the milk of a camel (a modern-day Cleopatra). She went to the local Zoo. She managed to steal a camel (where else can you find a camel when you need one?). She proceeded to transport it back to her house where she realized that the camel's name was "Otto."

These stories have a common denominator. They are a humorous look at stupid things people will do when they envy what other people have. For most of these criminals, they went after money. They probably envied the "easy" life that people with lots of money live.

Jonathan H. Wilson

The woman with the camel envied the smooth skin and good looks that the women in Oil of Olay commercials portrayed.

What is not funny are some of the following excerpts from various articles:

Leo Wilson, Jr., 16, was shot to death for his Nike sneakers and satin sports jacket.

Wheatley High School junior, Adam Joseph Martin, 18, gave haircuts to neighborhood kids to earn enough to buy his new $125 Nike athletic shoes last week. Saturday night, staring down the barrel of a 9mm pistol on a Houston street, he handed over his prized possessions to two robbers who fatally shot him anyway.

The people that committed both of these murders were after a pair of shoes made by Nike. It is incredible what envy will drive people to do. Why do so many people want to rob banks? Why do people kill each other? Why do spouses abuse each other in marriage? Why do children kill each other over a pair of shoes? Why do we tend to hurt those that we love?

Why do we hurt others? Not all, but much of the time we hurt people because we envy them.

I. We hurt people because we envy them.

a. We want what they have. James 4:2, "You want what you don't have, you long for what others have." Verse 1, "What is causing quarrels and fights among you? Isn't it the whole army of evil desires within you?" Here is a phrase I heard long ago, and it is so true: The Lord wants us to use things and love people, we tend to love things and use people."

b. We envy what which makes us feel good. Verse 3, "You want only what will give you pleasure." The Greek word in Verse 1 for "desires" is the word "hedone." It is from this term that we get the word "hedonism." It means "living for pleasure." Now that sounds sinful and evil doesn't it? But, you know what? It doesn't have to be that way. In fact, God wants us to be living for pleasure—only His pleasure. If we do, He will in turn give us unsurpassed joy—joy that will make our lives a living pleasure. A classmate of mine in Seminary, John Piper, has written a book entitled Desiring God. In the book he describes the idea of how "God wants us to become Christian hedonists." The Lord wants us to live for godly pleasures, but we have twisted them for selfish purposes. James is saying we have taken a good and godly desire for pleasure, desire that He has planted in us, and corrupted it. James describes this disturbing characteristic to corruption in Verse 2, "When you want something and don't get it you kill and covet, but you cannot have what you want. You quarrel and fight." This is why "envy" is found in the Bible as one of the "Seven Deadly Sins."

II. What is envy?

•Webster s Dictionary: Envy: A feeling of antagonism towards someone because of some good which he is enjoying but which one does not have oneself&a coveting for oneself of the good which someone else is enjoying.

•Vine s Greek: Envy is the feeling of displeasure produced by witnessing or hearing of the advantage or prosperity of others. This evil sense always attaches to this word&envy desires to deprive another of what he has.

•Christian psychologist, Dr. Gary Collins: To envy is to want something which belongs to another person.

•Envy is saying, I like what you ve got, I don t like the fact that you have it, and I want it!!!

I read a story of a 2nd grader who had collected a fair amount of money from the "tooth fairy." Every time she lost a tooth, they would put the tooth under her pillow and in the morning Rachel would find $2 under the pillow. Two dollars is a lot of money for a 2nd grader, at least, until she discovered that her best friend got $10 from the tooth fairy per tooth. Rachel then asked her friend's mother, "Mrs. Kraft, would you mind doing me a favor? Would you please call my Mom and tell her which tooth fairy you use?" This little girl had lost her contentment. Why? Because she had fallen prey to one of the most devious thieves known to man, a thief that robs more Christians of joy and satisfaction in life than any other feeling that I can think of—I call it "the envy trap." A 2nd grader with $2 in her pocket should be thrilled, but suddenly that was not enough. Why? Because she was envious of her friend who got $10 per tooth.

Jonathan H. Wilson

Envy is the emotion of a child who throws a temper tantrum when a brother or sister has something they want. Envy is the emotion we feel when we hear the news of someone hitting a 600 million-dollar jackpot. It is the emotion we feel when someone less deserving is successful while we struggle to barely make ends meet.

Let's put envy at a higher level. What is the real cause of the 9-11 attack? Is it not hatred, hatred for Americans because of envy for what Americans have? James is, I believe, saying that envy is the cause of much fighting, whether it is in marriages between spouses, children, or adult siblings. I would also venture to say it is the cause of much fighting in the political system. Certainly much of political infighting and positioning in Washington is caused by envy. It certainly causes much of the infighting in churches, and many institutions, schools as well as between countries in the world. Think about business wars that are caused by envy. Since 9-11, the only major airline that seems to have been making money was Southwest. All the other big carriers were swimming in red ink and have either declared bankruptcy or are thinking about it in order to avoid their creditors. So, in an atmosphere where most airlines are struggling to survive, Southwest's employees have relative job security. Yet, if you recall, some of the workers in one of its unions threatened to strike for higher wages because comparable employees in some of those failing airlines that were about to go bankrupt were making more per hour than they were. Does anyone besides me see the insanity of that? These union workers were not content because somebody else, workers in a failing airline were getting more than they were. It is natural to compare ourselves to others, but if it turns to envy, it becomes a sin. James' emphasis in this passage is what happens when we can't get our way. What are the consequences of our frustrated desires and how it leads to conflict—even murder if allowed to run its natural course unimpeded.

III. What is the impact of envy?

The impact of envy is the frustrated desire of a person or people to have more than what they already have, whether in position or possession. That hedonism leads to war and destruction whether it is on a small scale or large scale.

Take for example World War II. Why did it start? Basically because one man, Adolph Hitler, wanted to rule the world. His own selfish desire, which became the desire of Germany, threw the entire world

The Good News About Hard Times

into a devastating war. Selfish desire is liable to happen anywhere. During a certain church business meeting, the church leadership informed the church that they had consulted with an interior decorator that had helped them select very nice beige-colored carpet. Everyone seemed pleased with the selection, everyone except one gentleman who stood up and remarked that the church had always had red carpet, ever since he attended as a boy. He didn't want to change that now and was unwilling to accept that decision. He began shouting that he would "...never attend the church again" if they went against his desire to have red carpet. Soon, several others stood up to express their support, saying they, too, liked the red carpet and where did the church leadership have the right to make these decisions without consulting them first? This was important, after all. Now, people on both sides of this issue were making their desires known and the meeting erupted into a verbal argument, which lead into other areas in which selfish concerns were expressed. Because of the meeting, the church eventually split and many of the families no longer talk to each other at all. Why the conflict? James tells us—selfish desires and envy. What are the consequences? Wars, church splits, divorces, hurt feelings, fights, worthless arguments, saying things that shouldn't have been said, do not make a pretty picture any way you look at it. Let's look more closely at how envy effects us, personally.

Envy cripples our:

a. Ability to examine ourselves. We see it in the story of Cain and Abel. When God accepted the offering given to him and rejected the offering given by Cain, it made Cain very angry. Envy began to stew and boil in Cain's heart. The Lord warned Cain of this brooding emotion. Genesis 4:6-7, "Then the Lord said to Cain, 'Why are you so angry? Why is your face downcast? If you do what is right, will you not be accepted? But if you do not do what is right, sin is crouching at your door; (listen carefully) it desires to have you, but you must master it.'" Instead of heeding God's warning and examining himself, Cain let his envy consume him until he killed Abel, "I like what you've got, I don't like the fact that you have it and I want it!" How many of you have ever said, "Gee, how come God answers your prayers but not mine?" When you say that, envy has planted its seed in your heart. If you are not careful it will blossom and consume you. You have failed to examine the true motive of your prayers. James 4:3, "When you ask you do not receive because you ask with wrong motives that you may spend what you get on your pleasures." There are those that envy the so-called perfect family when they are in the midst of the breakdown of their own family. Those are the times when that envious person must examine himself or herself as to what they are doing in their own family. The reason envy is so dangerous is because it leads the person in an ever downward spiral and because it cripples the ability to examine ourselves—everything wrong or hurtful thing we do seems to be justified. "I like what you've got, I don't like the fact that you have it and I want it." Envy cripples!

b. Trust in God. Joseph and his brother are a good example. Genesis 37:11, his brothers were jealous of him and they did not trust in God, but in their own selfish desires. One of the saddest things that happens to a person is when their envy leads them to feel insecure. With envy you start taking things into your own hands instead of letting God take control of all things. Envy cripples!

c. Relationships—causing us to hurt loved ones. Talk about a downward spiral! Not only was there strife in the relationship between Joseph and his brothers, but also strife among the brothers themselves as they would have to live with their actions for the rest of their lives. And, not only among the brothers themselves but also in their relationship with their father, Jacob. This burden was only broken by Joseph's willingness to forgive many years later. Envying others leads to bitterness in our talk, an abruptness in our actions—backbiting, gossiping, and slander. Envy can take you from being a close friend to being a bitter enemy. It can break up families, tear churches apart, and ruin communities. A Greek proverb: As rust corrupts iron, so envy corrupts man.

d. Respect for authority/leaders. Aaron and Moses are a good example. Numbers 12:2-3, "Has the Lord spoken only through Moses?' They asked. 'Hasn't he also spoken through us?' And the Lord heard this." The Lord was very much aware of their envy. Psalm 106:16, "In the camp they grew envious of Moses and of Aaron who was consecrated to the Lord. And the Lord was not pleased."

d. Diminishes ability to enjoy what we have. In Esther 5:11, "Haman boasted to them about his vast wealth, his many sons, and all the ways the king had honored him and how he had elevated him above the other nobles and officials. Verse 12, "And that's not all, Haman added, "I'm the only person Queen Esther invited to accompany the king to the banquet she gave. And she has invited me along with the

The Good News About Hard Times

king tomorrow. Verse 13, "But all this gives me no satisfaction as long as I see that Jew Mordecai sitting at the king's gate." Envy diminished his ability to enjoy the blessing he already had. Moody told the fable of an eagle who was envious. Dwight L. Moody once told the fable of an eagle who was envious of another that could fly better than he could. One day the bird blinded by envy saw a sportsman with a bow and arrow and said to him, "I wish you would bring down that eagle up there." The man said he would if he had some more fine feathers for his arrow. So the jealous eagle pulled a few out of his wing. The arrow was shot, but it didn't quite reach the rival bird because he was flying too high. The first eagle pulled out more and then more feathers, until he had pulled out so many that he himself couldn't fly. The archer took advantage of the situation, turned around, and killed the helpless bird. Dr. Moody's point was that envy not only cripples our ability to enjoy what we have but also to be thankful for what we have. How many of us have ever said, "If only I had…" Yet, in saying this we forget that the living standards we are privileged to enjoy in this country are considered luxurious to someone living in most countries of the world, such as Rwanda, China, Ethiopia, and many others.

f. Harms our relationship with God. In these Verses, James tells us why our desires are not fulfilled. If we don't pray, we don't ask God. We look to the wrong source. We look to people rather than God to fulfill our needs. He says, "I'll meet your needs, just pray." But, when we do pray we usually pray with the wrong motive. We ask for things in a selfish way. The Bible says that everything I need, God has promised to provide. He'll meet our needs according to His riches. But instead of praying, we look to ourselves or others to work things out. We'd rather do it our way; we sing like "Old' Blue Eyes" Frank Sinatra used to pridefully sing, "I did it my way." Prayerlessness in itself is evidence of pride. James said that we would have a lot more peace if we just prayed more. We'd have a lot less to worry about, a lot more peace if we just prayed more. Remember the old hymn, "Oh what peace we often forfeit, oh what needless pain we bear, all because we do not carry everything to (Whom?) …everything to God in prayer."

In the next verses, James talks about conflict with God. Pride not only causes conflict with other people, but it causes conflict with God. Verse 6, "God opposes the proud but gives grace to the humble." God declares war on selfishness. Have you noticed that God has a way of allowing difficult circumstances to pop our pride? Just about the time you think, "I've got it all together, I don't need God," He puts you in your place? To be in opposition to God is to be in a dangerous place. You're on a collision course with God and there is no way you're going to win. Verse 6 says, "God opposes the proud." Could it be any clearer? That is not a good position in which to be.

IV. The cure for envy

Friends, if there is envy anywhere in your life, listen carefully to what God says is the cure. James 4:8-9. "...in order to come near to God we must..."

a. Pray. James has already emphasized the importance of coming to God in prayer. He has already told us that God is the giver or all good gifts; therefore, if we desire something we should turn to Him. But, there is a hitch. Someone reading James' letter might at this point have said, "Wait a minute, James, I do pray. In fact, I pray every day and God hasn't answered my prayers. The guy down the street has a new tunic, and I want one. I have been praying faithfully every day for a month now and God hasn't given me one, yet." That may seem like a realistic complaint at first and I'll bet that everyone in this room has had that kind of complaint at one time or another. Have you ever prayed for something really hard and never got it? You prayed and prayed, but God didn't provide it for you. As a result you complained to Him and to others about how God does not answer your prayers. Have you ever done this? What does James say about your complaint? James says that we are praying with wrong motives. You ask for something out of your own desire for your own way. You don't really care what God's will is in the situation, you just want things more comfortable for you. You say, "God help me to pay off my financial debt." But the debt remains. Did it ever occur to you that what God's will might be in that situation; perhaps he wants you to be more careful with your finances. Maybe, just maybe, He wants you to rethink your finances. Maybe it will cause you to be less materialistic and rely on Him more. No, we somehow think that God has some magic wand that we can force into action whenever the situations of life become uncomfortable or whenever we would like more of something. It doesn't work that way. God is not your Easter Bunny or Santa Claus, or Genie in a bottle. He is the Sovereign God of the universe, and He has a plan. Life isn't about being comfortable! It is about desiring God's will and seeking to please Him so that He can fill your life with joy and make it a pleasure to live.

The Good News About Hard Times

b. Seek forgiveness. James says, "Wash your hands, purify your heart." Our hands represent our conduct and our hearts represent our attitudes. He is saying to clean up your act, your conduct, and your attitudes. Verse 9, "Let there be tears for the wrong you have done." Here is James' challenge for us: He wants us to be constantly examining ourselves to that we can rid ourselves of ungodly desires. For, if we don't, not only are we in trouble ourselves, but those around us will be negatively affected as well. James said that left unchecked, self-centeredness and envy would cause disorder, wars, and evil of every kind.

When we receive the Lord's Supper, spend some time in quiet self-examination. Paul told us before receiving the Lord's supper to examine ourselves for areas of unconfessed sin, for areas of ungodly motives. During this time, confess to Him any sin that the Holy Spirit brings to your mind, such as the desire for material things, and the envy of those who have things, or position, or family that you feel you ought to have, but don't. Confess that you often look to people to fulfill your needs rather than God. Look carefully into your inner life and conflicts that you have had. If you have hurt someone, ask God's forgiveness, and then at the right time seek him or her out and ask their forgiveness. Watch and see how your relationships with people and the church improve. Watch and see God work in your life. In order for that to happen, we must humble ourselves.

c. Humble yourself. Verse 6, "He gives grace to the humble." Could it be any more clear? When we receive communion it is the opportunity to wash our hands. To come before God with repentance, faith, and reformation. We are all sinners, and in order to experience the healing presence of God, we must be cleansed.

Jesus has provided the wash basin—the cross. It was His sacrificial bloodshed on a cross that gives us the opportunity to be released from the bondage of sin and the chains of guilt. We must lay our envious thoughts bare before the cross and say, "Lord, forgive me." If you humble yourself not only will God give you grace, but Verse 10 says, "He will lift you up."

My friends, God doesn't want to keep us on the ground, held down by the shackles of sin. He wants us to be free to soar like an eagle. He wants to be the wind beneath our wings. However, to do so we must first humble ourselves. Verse 10, "Humble yourselves in the eyes of the Lord…he will lift you up."

{"Everything we give on this side of Eternity is being accredited to our account on the other side of eternity"

Luke 16:9 "So, I say to you, use worldly wealth to gain friends for yourself so that when it is gone you will be welcomed into eternal dwellings"}

"All it takes is 57 cents"

"Growing God's Kingdom"

Book of James - Chapter 13

James 5:1-6

I recently heard a story about several guys who were in the locker room of a private exercise club. They were all talking when a cell phone lying on the bench rang. One man picked it up without hesitation and the following conversation ensued:

-"Hello?"

-"Honey, it's me!"

-"Oh, hi dear!"

-"I'm at the mall two blocks from the club. I saw a beautiful mink coat. It is absolutely gorgeous! Can I buy it? It's only $1,500."

-"Well, okay, if you like it that much."

-"Thanks! Oh, and I also stopped by the Mercedes dealership and saw the new models. I saw one I really liked. I spoke with the salesman and he gave me a great price."

-"How much?"

-"Only $60,000!"

-"Okay, but for that price I want it with all the options."

-"Great! But before we hang up, there's something else. It might seem like a lot, but, well, I stopped by to see the real estate agent this morning and I saw the house we had looked at last year. It's on sale! Remember? It's the beachfront property with the pool and the English garden."

-"How much are they asking?"

Jonathan H. Wilson

-"Only $450 million! It's really quite a bargain and we have that much in the bank accounts to cover it."

-"Well then, go ahead and buy it, but make an offer for only $4.2 million, okay?"

-"Okay, sweetie. Thanks! I'll see you later! I love you!"

-"I love you, too."

At that, the man hung up the cell phone, closed the flap, and raised it in the air. "Does anyone know whose cell phone this is?" Money is easy to talk about when it is someone else's, but not so easy when it is our own.

Many people wrongly believe that the Bible teaches that it is wrong to be wealthy. They think that the Bible says, "Money is the root of all evil." It actually says, "The love of money is the root of all evil." God is not opposed to wealth; in fact, many of the people in the Bible were extremely wealthy. In our terms, Abraham was probably a millionaire.

Job was the wealthiest man of his time. David and Solomon were both the wealthiest men of their time. We know that Barnabas made a lot of money because he was able to give it to the church. Joseph of Arimathea, the man who gave Jesus his tomb, was extremely wealthy. So God is not opposed to wealth. However, God is very much opposed to the misuse and abuse of wealth. In the New Testament times, there was no such thing as middle class. The people in the entire New Testament times were either very rich or very poor. You were either a "have" or a "have not." The system caused the rich to get richer and the poor to get poorer. The rich tended to manipulate and oppress the poor people who were continually abused.

James' thoughts in James 5:1-6, are directed at wealthy unbelievers who were exploiting the poor, many of whom were in the church. Though these persons were the callused unbelieving rich, the message also meant to benefit the church. James understood the human tendency to envy the "rich and the famous." James' terrifying description of judgment awaiting these rich countrymen is meant to encourage the exploited poor. They need to be patient for judgment is coming.

The Good News About Hard Times

James lashes out at the ungodly use of money by the wealthy. He gives a rebuke, probably one of the most negative passages in the entire New Testament. He devastates them with four specific abuses of which they were guilty. Although we may not commit these sins to the same degree, this passage is a healthy warning to us to make sure that no matter how much money we have, we use it wisely. James' words are a wake-up call to the rich.

Several years ago, a Rotarian magazine tells about a bounty of $5,000 offered for each wolf captured alive. It turned Sam and Jed into fortune hunters. Day and night they scoured the mountains and forests looking for their valuable prey. Exhausted one night, they fell asleep dreaming of their potential fortune. Suddenly, Sam awoke to see that about 50 wolves with flaming eyes and bared teeth surrounded them. He nudged his friend and said, "Jed, wake up! We're rich!" Today, James would say to us, "My words are a wake-up call to the rich."

Today, we're going to look at the wrong and right uses of wealth. James mentions four common abuses of wealth. First, let's look at the wrong uses of wealth and how to avoid them. Then, we'll look at the right uses.

I. The Wrong Use of Wealth

A. Don't hoard. (Verse 3) "You have hoarded wealth in these last days." God is telling us not to stockpile wealth just for the sake of having it. We've all seen, for the past few weeks, how Saddam has hoarded wealth to the detriment of his people, and he will face judgment for it. Why? God wants money in circulation. Saddam stockpiled in numerous places, perhaps billions of dollars. He had all these buildings full of money. We've heard of people like that. People who hoard every penny they have, but never have the joy of spending it or giving it away. There is the true story of John G. Wendel and his sisters. Even though they had received a huge inheritance from their parents, they were some of the most miserly people of all time. They spent very little and did all they could to hoard their wealth for themselves. John was able to influence five of his six sisters never to marry, and they lived in the same house in New York City for 50 years. When the last sister died in 1931, her estate was valued at more than $100 million. Yet, her only dress was one that she had made herself and had worn for 25 years. The

Jonathan H. Wilson

Wendels had such a compulsion to hold on to their possessions that they lived like paupers. Even worse, they were the kind of person that Jesus referred to "...who lays up treasure for himself, and is not rich toward God." (Luke 12/21) James views this type of hoarding as obscene because it corrupts and corrodes life. In New Testament times, you could hoard wealth in three ways: stockpile food, collect clothing, and gather precious jewels or metals. That is the way people showed off their wealthy. If you had money you would show it off by having lots of food, fancy clothes, gold, silver, and jewels (gold-plated AK-47's). In Verses 2 and 3, James says, "Everything you've gotten has spoiled or rotted, or corroding, rusting, or moth eaten." He is saying that which we attempt to accumulate, deteriorates. God doesn't want us to collect stuff; he wants us to put it into circulation.

B. Don't get wealth unfairly. (Verse 4) James is in effect saying, "You have condemned and raided innocent men, and they are powerless to stop you." (Verse 6, PH) There were no labor laws in the New Testament days. James is in effect saying, "Don't use dishonest means to rip off people. Pay them what they are worth."

C. Don't steal it. (Verse 4) God is not only concerned with what we have, but how we got it. Don't steal it. Don't use dishonest means to rip off people. There are a lot of dishonest ways to get money. Look at the looting that goes on in some cities when problems break out. A few dishonest looters have bought into the lie of the "lifestyles of the rich and famous."

D. Don't be dishonest. (Verse 4) God demands we make money honestly and fairly. Proverbs 21:20, "A fortune can be made from cheating but there's a curse that goes with it." What about the Fox news man who was covering the touring of Saddam's palatial palaces and walked off with over a dozen paintings! He'll probably never have a responsible position again. There is a curse that goes with dishonesty.

E. Don't waste it. (Verse 5) Here, James is blasting these guys for how they waste their money. What about that extra food that has gone rotten in the refrigerator? We stockpile so much food from Costco that we could feed an army for six months. However, from another angle we are doing research. Actually, we are creating whole new life forms in the back of our refrigerators.

The Good News About Hard Times

F. Don't manipulate with it. (Verse 6) James is talking about how we use money for influence. He says that we should not abuse money. Wealth gives us a lot more than simply more buying ability. Richard Foster, in his excellent book, Money, Sex, and Power, says, "Money has a lot more power than simply buying power. When you have money, it gives you more influence, authority." It is human to tend to listen to people who make money, more so than to people who are poor. Now this is not necessarily good or bad. Some use it to influence people. Often, for very poor reasons, they use it to manipulate and finance campaigns. Christians ought to recognize that money has influence, and use it for good. The point that James is making in this passage is that "we ought to use our affluence for good influence." James says that we should recognize that it is powerful and not abuse it, but use it in good ways.

II. The Right Use of Wealth

A. The wise person saves.

1. Why save? (Proverbs 21:20), "The wise man saves for the future, but the foolish man spends whatever he gets." Proverbs 21:20 (LB) This is the principle that the Bible says we ought to save money faithfully. The average American only saves 4% of his income. The average European saves 16% of his income. The average Japanese person saves 25% of his income. Why do we save so little in America? I think it is because we live for today. I want it now, whether or not I can afford it. I'll put it on my credit card. God says the wise person saves and invests his money. Jesus told a number of parables, and over half deal with money. He talked more about money than he did about heaven or hell. Jesus talks positively about investments—how the wise man invested his money and the unwise man didn't invest his money. The master came back and said, "You're wicked." It's wicked not to make our money work for us. A very wealthy man has as his motto: Use it up, wear it out, make it do, or do without. What is the purpose of saving? Here is where the Bible differs in a big way from the world's thinking. The world thinks you save money for security. I really think that Saddam thought that his millions of dollars made him secure. The problem is that there is no such thing as absolute security. No matter how much money you've got, you could lose it instantly. Bunker Hunt, a billionaire was quoted in Time Magazine, saying that he lost over one billion dollars. Hunt said, matter of factly, "A billion dollars ain't what it used to be."

Jonathan H. Wilson

You can lose it no matter how much you make. No matter what kind of job you have. You could break a leg, get sick, the economy can turn even worse, or the place could burn down. In order to have security you have to put your security in something that cannot be taken away from you. Everything in your life can be taken away from you—your family, your money, your reputation, everything! There is only one thing that cannot be taken away from us and that is our relationship to Jesus Christ. I've got to put my security in Christ and not a passbook account, CD's, gold, or stock. We don't save like the world saves, simply for security. Paul said in Philippians 4:19, "My God shall supply all your needs." That's security!

2. It allows us to help others. Charles Colson told the following story in an address at Reformed Theological Seminary in Jackson, Mississippi: 'In 1985, I was on the Bill Buckley television program, talking about restitution and criminal justice. A few days later I got a call from Jack Eckerd, a businessman from Florida, the founder of the Eckerd Drug chain, the second largest drug chain in America. "He saw me on television and asked me to come to Florida. He agreed Florida had a criminal justice crisis, would I come down and do something about it? And, we did. We went around the State of Florida advocating criminal justice reforms and everywhere we would go Jack Eckerd would introduce me to the crowds and says, "This is Chuck Colson, I met him on Bill Buckley's television program. He's born again; I'm not. I wish I were.' Then he would sit down. About a year went by and I kept pestering Jack Eckerd about faith in Jesus. Eventually, one day he read some things including the story of Watergate and the Resurrection out of my book, Loving God, and decided that Jesus was, in fact, resurrected from the dead. He called me up to tell me he believed. When he got through telling me what he believed I said, "You're born again!" He said, "Marvelous!" The first thing he did was to walk into one of his drugstores and walked down through the bookshelves where he saw Playboy and Penthouse. He had seen it there many times before, but it never bothered him before. Now he saw them with new eyes. He'd become a Christian. He went back to his office. He called in his president. He said, "Take Playboy and Penthouse out of my stores." The president said, "You can't mean that, Mr. Eckerd. We make $3 million a year on them." Eckerd said, "Take them out of my stores." And in 17,000 stores across America, those magazines were removed from the shelves because a man had given his life to Christ. Colson called

Jack Eckerd and ask, "Did you do that because of your commitment to Christ?" He said, "Why else would I give away $3 million? The Lord wouldn't let me off the hook." Isn't that marvelous? God wouldn't let me off the hook.

And what happened after that is a wonderful sequel and a wonderful demonstration of what happens in our culture today. Jack Eckerd wrote a letter to all the other drugstore operators, all the other chains, and he said, "I've taken them out of my store, why don't you take them out of yours?" Nobody answered him. So he wrote them more letters. Then Eckerd's Drugs began to get floods of people coming in to buy things because they'd taken Playboy and Penthouse out. So People's Drug Store, and then Dart Drugs, and then Revco removed them from their shelves. While the pornography commission in Washington was debating what to do about pornography, across America, one by one, stores were removing them. The 7-11 chairman, who sits on Jack Eckerd's board finally gave in and 5,000 7-11 Stores, removed them. In 12 months, 11,000 retail outlets in America removed Playboy and Penthouse, not because somebody passed a law, but because God wouldn't let one of His wealthy men off the hook. That's what brings change. Isn't that an amazing story! Jack Eckerd risked losing $3 million per year. That's a great testimony about how someone strong in faith in Christ and with great wealth can do.

3. It works for you. (Proverbs 13:11) "Dishonest money dwindles away, but he who gathers money little by little makes it grow."

B. How much wealth can you make?

1. Why do we save? The Christian saves for stewardship reasons, not for security reasons. Three reasons for saving:

a. It prevents us from impulse buying. We don't spend money on foolish impulses. If we're not saving it, the tendency is to spend it as soon as you get it. You'll see things you want and buy it and you really don't need. Proverbs 21:20, "The wise man saves for the future, but the foolish man spends whatever he gets."

b. It allows us to be able to help other people when they have a need. We save in order to help others. Many times Patty and I have used a little extra money we have to help other people in need and that has been a blessing. We've also had the blessing of receiving from people who have helped us in a time of need.

c. It works for you rather than you working for your money. That is the principle of investment. When you're saving your money it is being invested wisely, it is working for you instead of you working for it. Proverbs 14:23, "Hard work brings a profit; mere talk leads to poverty." Over and over again in Scripture, the Bible teaches the value of hard work. It is a legitimate, honest way to increase your income by making money, honestly, through work. If you talk all the time, dream, and plan get-rich-quick schemes you're not going to prosper in life. God approves of work as a means to wealth. Proverbs 11:16 (GN) "If you're lazy you'll never get what you're after. But if you work hard, you can get a fortune." What matters to God is not so much how much money you make but how you make it.

C. How do we use our wealth for God?

1. We are to give money generously. Proverbs 11:24-25, "It is possible to give away and become richer. It is also possible to hold on too tightly and lose everything. Yes, the generous man shall be rich. By watering others, he waters himself." This principle is taught over and over again in Scripture. Give and it will be given unto you. Just like seeds, the more we sow the more we reap. The root of the word "miserable" is "miser". When I'm a miser, when I hold on and I'm not a generous person with my giving, then I am miserable. But, if I learn to give I'll be a very happy person. No matter how wealthy I've become, I'm not financially free until I've learned to give. In order to live abundantly, I've got to give abundantly. Here's a thought from an unknown author: "When it comes to giving, some people have sclerosis of the giver." Back to the question of how much money can I make as a Christian, legitimately? There is no set limit to the amount of money you make. Scripture says you can make as much money as you can in your lifetime as long as you meet these four qualifications. Earn as much as you can, as long as it does not:

a. Hurt your health. Some people literally work themselves to death. They amass a personal fortune then have a heart attack. In our society, it seems like the workaholics are the heroes. Scripture teaches that health must always take priority over wealth. Proverbs 23:4, "Do not wear yourselves out to get rich. Have the wisdom to show restraint." I heard a joke this past week about a young man

The Good News About Hard Times

who was driving his BMW around a curve when he realized the car was out of control and about to plummet over a cliff. The young man jumped out, but his left arm was severed from his body. He stood there looking down at his burning BMW and said, "Oh, no! My car! My car!" A man who had stopped to help said, "Mister, you have just lost your left arm, and you're crying about your car?" The young man looked down and said, "Oh no, my Rolex watch!" We're like the donkey that has the carrot extended before it on a stick. The donkey sees the carrot and wants it, so the donkey moves toward it, but the carrot moves, too. The carrot is always there, promising to fill the appetite. But what it promises, it does not deliver. The point is, don't work yourself to death like a dumb donkey. Earn as much as you can if you don't:

b. Hurt your family. Recently, John Paul Getty, Jr., died. The Los Angeles Times said, "His life was a parable about the effect money can have, both for good and as a curse, on those who have it. By all accounts, Getty was obsessed by money. He once said, 'If you can count your money, you are not really rich.'" The Times said he was a cold father to his five sons. One died of a brain tumor, another by suicide, and he didn't even attend the marriage of another son who married a childhood sweetheart. The son never set foot inside the Getty Center in Los Angeles." How many homes have fallen apart because kids are being ignored while parents are too busy making money to buy things for the kids? We can get so busy making a living that we can forget to make a life. Make as much as you can as long as you don't hurt other people.

c. Hurt other people. This is the exact opposite of Saddam's view: get all you can, can all you get, sit on the can, and spoil the rest. Look at the wealth in those Iraq bungalows, while people all around were starving and in poverty. That kind of wealth hurt millions of people. Make all you can as long as you don't hurt your spiritual life.

d. Hurt your spiritual life. In 3 John 2, "Beloved I wish that you may prosper and be in health even as your soul prospers." John says, I pray that God will bless you financially as you are blessed spiritually. This is the principle of balance. As long as my spiritual growth is progressing at the level as my financial prosperity, go ahead and make whatever you can. God wants us to be in balance. Here is a question for you: If your income were at the same degree as your walk with the Lord, would you be a millionaire, a pauper,

Jonathan H. Wilson

or somewhere in between? God wants us to have balance. You have financial goals. Do you have spiritual goals, too? What about relational goals?

C. How to use our wealth for God. The Bible says we are to spend money wisely. The Scripture says, "The plans of the diligent lead to profit as sure as haste leads to poverty." We spend 16 years in school, learning how to make money but not six weeks learning how to spend it wisely. How many agree with this statement: It is easier to get into debt than to get out of debt. Buy now; pay later. Only 162 easy payments! I've never had an easy payment. They are all difficult. The number one reason for financial pressure is not that we don't make enough money, but we don't spend it wisely. We make good incomes in America, but we're never going to have enough money unless we know how to spend it wisely. The more your income goes up, it seems your expenses also go up. Our yearning capacity always tends to exceed our earning capacity. How do you spell relief? B-u-d-g-e-t. What is a budget? Planned spending. Telling your money where you want it to go rather than wondering where it went. The wise man plans. The plans of the diligent lead to profit as sure as haste leads to poverty. The opposite of budget spending is impulse buying. I see it, I want it, and I'm going to buy it.

1. Give money generously. Proverbs 11:25, "It is possible to give away and become richer! It is also possible to hold on too tightly and lose everything. Yes, the generous man shall be rich. By watering others, he waters himself." You see, we can afford to be generous. A man in New York City had a wife who had a favorite cat. She loved the cat. She stroked it, combed its fur, fed it, and pampered it. The husband hated the cat. He was allergic to cat hair; he detested the smell of the litter box; he couldn't stand the scratching on the furniture; and, he couldn't get a good night's sleep because the cat kept jumping on the bed. Finally one day when his wife was out of town for the weekend, he put the cat in a bag with some rocks, dumped it in the Hudson River. When his wife returned and could not find her cat, she was overwhelmed with grief. Her husband thoughtfully said, "Look honey, I know how much that cat meant to you. I'm going to put an ad in the paper and give a reward of $1000 to anyone who finds the cat." Sadly, No cat showed up, so a few days later he said, "Honey, you mean more to me than anything on earth. If that cat is precious to you, it is precious to me. I'll tell you what I'll do. I'll buy another ad and raise the reward. We'll increase the reward to $2,000. A friend

saw the advertisement and exclaimed, "You must be nuts; there isn't a cat on earth that is worth a $2000." The man replied, "Well, when you know what I know, you can afford to be very generous."

If we have any inkling of what it means to be part of God's kingdom, we can afford to be generous. We can be generous because we can't out-give God.

2. Invest in Heaven's treasures. Matthew 6:20, "Store up for yourselves treasure in heaven..." God wants us to make money honestly, save it faithfully, spend it wisely. Luke 12:15, "And he said unto them, take heed and beware of covetousness: for a man's life consists not in the abundance of the things which he possesses." This is the opposite of what the world teaches us. If there is one message that comes to us in ten thousand seductive voices, it is the message of our country and our century that life does consist of things. You can see it on a hundred billboards as you drive down the highway. It is the message from the sponsor on television. It is sung to you in jingles on radio. It is blared at you in four-color ads in the newspapers. You've heard many people say, "You can't take it with you." That's very true, but you can send it on ahead. The Bible says, "Store up for yourselves treasure in Heaven." Matthew 6:20, "Where your treasure is your heart will be also." I heard about the guy that died and got to heaven. He saw all the big mansions and then one little shack. He said, "Is that where I'm supposed to live? Why?" Answer: "That's all the building material you sent ahead." How do you send it on ahead? How do you store up treasure in heaven? The only way you can store up treasure in heaven is by investing it in people who are going there. There is only one thing that is going to last forever in heaven—people who know the Lord. Everything else is going to burn up at the judgment. Invest your time and money in getting the word of God to people. When you invest in getting people into heaven, then you will store up treasures in heaven. How do you do that? How do you invest in people? Jesus told a parable that illustrates this. In Luke 16, Jesus told a story that shocked a lot of people because he used a crook as an example to make a spiritual point. Luke 16:1, Jesus told the disciples, "There was a rich man whose manager was accused of wasting his possessions. So he called in the man and said, 'What's this I hear about you? Give an account of your management, because you can no longer be a manager.' The manager said to himself, 'What am I going to do now? My master is taking away my job. [He got fired for being dishonest.]

Jonathan H. Wilson

I'm not strong enough to dig and I'm too ashamed to beg. I know what I'll do so that when I lose my job people will welcome me into their homes.' So he called in each one of his master's debtors and asked the first one, 'How much do you owe my master?' "800 gallons of olive oil,' he replied. The manager told him, 'Quick, take your bill. Set down quickly and make it 400.' Then he asked the second, 'How much do you owe?' '1000 bushels of wheat,' he replied. 'Take your bill and make it 800.' [He's being dishonest again simply to make friends with these guys.] The master commended his dishonest manager because he had acted shrewdly. Jesus told a story about a crook and used the guy as an example. He didn't commend his dishonesty, But the master said, that really was pretty smart. The people of darkness of this world are more shrewd in their dealings with their own kind than the people of light. People in the world realize the influence that money has, but they often use it for the wrong reason. Then he says, "So, I say to you, use worldly wealth to gain friends for yourself so that when it is gone you will be welcomed into eternal dwellings." Jesus is saying that when you use money and invest it in people who come to know Christ, you are making friends for eternity. When you get to heaven, they'll say they are there because of you. You will be welcomed in. "You gave to a church that caused a missionary to come and tell me about the Lord" "I'm here because you gave," or "You gave for a building fund and I came to that church and came to know the Lord. "I'm in heaven because of you." Jesus says to use your affluence for good influence. Then, people will welcome you into eternal dwellings. Who is going to be the welcoming committee for you? Who is going to say, "I'm here because of you." This is what Jesus is talking about here. Everything we give on this side of eternity is being accredited to our account on the other side in eternity.

3. Give consistently, and give regularly. Luke 16:1-13, I Corinthians 16:2, "Giving is to be regular. It is to be consistent." I Corinthians 16:2, "On every Sunday, put aside something from what you have earned during the week, and use it for the offering. The amount depends on how much the Lord has helped you to earn." Giving is consistent, regular, and proportional. When we do, one of the greatest comments that can be made to us is the one Jesus will tell us when we join Him in heaven, "Well done, good and faithful servant." We need to let loose of our grip on our possessions, and let God take over. Corrie Ten Boom once said, "I have learned not

The Good News About Hard Times

to hold on to things in this life too tightly because it hurts when God pries my fingers loose from them." How true that is!

I close with this true story. A sobbing little girl stood near a small church entrance from which she had been turned away because it was overcrowded. "I can't go to Sunday school," she quietly sobbed to the pastor, as he passed by. Taking her by the hand, he found a special place for her inside the sanctuary. The child was so touched that she went to bed that night thinking of the children who had no special place to worship Jesus. A few years later, this child lay dead in one of the poor tenement buildings, and the parents called for the kindhearted pastor to make the funeral arrangements. Under her pillow he found a crumpled purse rummaged from the dump. In it were 57 pennies and a note scribbled in crude childish handwriting, "'his is to help build the little church bigger so more children can go to Sunday school." For two years she had saved for this offering of love. When the pastor read that note, he knew instantly what he would to. He took the note and the little cracked, red pocketbook to the pulpit for a visual, and he told the story of her unselfish love and devotion. He challenged his leaders to get raise enough money for the larger church. But that was not the end. In a short time a newspaper learned of the story and published it. A realtor read it and offered them a lot worth many thousands. When the church could not pay so much, he offered it for a modest figure and said he would take as a down payment exactly 57 cents. Checks came in the mail from far and wide. Within five years the little girl's gift had increased to $250,000. Her unselfish love had paid large dividends. Today, when you visit the city of Philadelphia, the city of brotherly love, look at Temple Baptist Church, with a seating capacity of 3300, also Temple University, where hundreds of students are trained. Look around also at the Good Samaritan Hospital and at the spacious Sunday school building, so that no child in that vicinity will ever need to be left outside when coming to Sunday school. If you were to tour that facility today, you would find, a slightly dated picture of the sweet face of the little girl whose 57 cents, so sacrificially saved, made such remarkable history.

{"Be patient and trust Him. Gods delays are not Gods denials. He may be slow, but he's never late."

James 5;11 "You have heard of Job's perseverance and have seen what the Lord finally brought about. The Lord is full of compassion and mercy"}

"Patience in Times of Suffering"

"What to do in the waiting room?"

Book of James - Chapter 14

James 5:7-12

Don't you wish this were a perfect world? In a perfect world, chocolate would have no calories. In a perfect world, procrastination would be honored as a virtue. In a perfect world, teenagers would rather clean their room than talk on the phone; politicians would pay us taxes; grandchildren on trips would say, "Grandma, isn't riding in the car fun?" and then they would promptly go to sleep. In a perfect world, candy would be considered a vegetable. Some women feel that in a perfect world, men would go through labor.

Unfortunately, we don't live in a perfect world. Therefore, we need to learn what James is talking about today. James writes in 5:7, "Dear brothers and sisters, you must be patient as you wait for the Lord's return." We all need patience in an imperfect world. That is why Paul said that one of the "fruit of the spirit" is patience. If you have the Holy Spirit in your life, one of the signs of His presence in your life is patience.

Let's talk about patience. Anyone here need to learn how to be more patient? The real impatient people are saying, "Get on with the message, you are wasting our time!" The Greek word for patience is "macro-thermos." The word, "macro" means big or long or slow; "thermos" means heat or energy or anger or wrath. Putting the two together means, "It takes a long time to heat up." You don't boil over quickly; slow to get angry.

Alexander the Great, in a fit of rage, struck and killed his favorite general. He proclaimed, in a famous phrase, "I have conquered the world, but I have not conquered my own soul." This brings to mind Proverbs 16:32, "It is better to be slow-tempered than famous; it is better to have self-control than to control an army." Anger, in itself, is not wrong or sinful. God was angry; Jesus was angry. Anger is not always wrong because God has given us the capacity to get angry, but it must be managed. It must be controlled. Anger, out of control, is extremely destructive to relationships, to careers, and to reputations. Thermos, under control, together with macro, or a very long fuse, can be a tremendous asset.

I. When to be patient.

a. When circumstances are beyond your control, are you patient? In our text, James used the farmer as an example of when circumstances are uncontrollable. Verse 7, "Be patient then, brothers, until the Lord's coming. See how the farmer waits for the land to yield its valuable crop and how patient he is for the autumn and spring rains." Part of the job description of being a farmer is that you do a lot of waiting—waiting to till the soil, waiting to plant, waiting to prune. Some factors we can control such as irrigation, bug spray, etc., but there are some factors over which the farmer has no control—weather, rain, heat, the economy, labor practices. If you don't have a lot of patience, don't be a farmer because you deal with a lot of uncontrollable factors. Some people are like the little school kid who plants a seed and pulls it up every day to see if it's growing. When circumstances get beyond our control, we still try to control it, don't we? How do we do that? By worrying! We think that worry will control a situation, but to worry about something you can control is "dumb!" However, to worry about something you can't control is ludicrous. Either way, we shouldn't worry. We need to have patience when circumstances are beyond our control.

b. When people are unchangeable. Are we patient when people are unchangeable? James gives us an example, "As an example of patience in the face of suffering, take the prophets who spoke in the name of the Lord." (Verse 11) What was the duty of the prophets? To help people change, to bring them back to God, to be different in their behavior, to repent, and go in a new direction. Have you noticed that some people resist change? When you make any little suggestion they take the opposite opinion. Some people, no matter what you say, will argue the opposite viewpoint. Do you have anybody in your life right now like that who refuses to change? They are difficult to live with; argue on both side of every issue. Joyce Landorf calls them "irregular people." They are people who only see things their own way. Psychologists call them borderline personalities. They may never change because they only see the world from one perspective. What are you going to do if people refuse to cooperate, to change? James says, "Don't let it ruin your life. Have patience."

The Good News About Hard Times

c. When problems are unexplainable. The classic example James gives us in Verse 11, "You have heard of Job's perseverance..." Job played in the super bowl of suffering. He won the championship. He was the wealthiest man in the world at that time. He had everything going for him but within a two-day period everything fell apart. He went bankrupt. His children were murdered. He got an incurable, deadly, and painful disease. You think you've got problems? He went from penthouse to the poorhouse in two days. He lost his family, his friends, and his finances. He was suffering materially, physically, socially—every which way, and he had a great support system. His wife, one day, came to him and said, "Why don't you just curse God and die!" She was consistently a nagger. God allowed Satan to take away everything in Job's life except a nagging wife. The worst part of Job's suffering was that he had absolutely no idea why it was happening. For 37 Chapters in the Book of Job, God doesn't even talk to him and tell him what is going on. Of all people, Job had the privilege to say, "Why me? Life is not fair!" That is true. God never said it would be fair. That is a lie our parents taught us. A lot of things in life just don't make sense. Do the right thing and the right thing will happen. Ultimately, yes...but right now...doubtful. I could give you a whole list of unfair things in my life and I'm sure you could, too. Yet, in spite of all the bad things and unexplained problems, Job maintained his faith.

II. Why be patient?

Important people want to be in control. If we have been through difficult circumstances in the past we tend to want to be in control in the future so that it doesn't happen again. Control is the one word that most characterizes an impatient person. When they say "jump" they want people to say, "How high?" They want to tell God, "God, now I want you to do this..." and, they want God to jump! They want to be in control of God, too. On the other hand, patience means that I will let somebody else be in control, I will abide under somebody else's control. The deeper question is, "Am I willing to let God be God, or do I want hi to be God on my terms when He plays by my rules?" "Okay, God, it is all right for you to be God IF you do what I want you to do. Then, I'll praise you. Then, I'll go to church, and then I will put my pledge in the offering plate as long as you do what I want you to do. But Lord, if you don't do what I want you to do, I'm out of here!" Who, really, is God in that conversation? Perhaps one of the most practical ways to see if somebody really lives under the

Lordship of Jesus Christ in their lives or whether it's just words, is their level of patience when things don't go according to their plans. An impatient person has to be in control. A patient person has learned to be patient.

a. Because God is in control

Three times in this passage James says the Lord is coming near, Jesus is coming back. That is the ultimate proof that God is in control. Nothing can stop it. The Bible talks more about Jesus' Second Coming than it does about his first coming. God is in control of history. History is His-story! To recognize that is a sign of spiritual maturity. James 1:2, "Consider it pure joy my brothers, whenever you have trials of many kinds, because you know that the testing of your faith develops patience, the ability to persevere to the finish." Biblical patience is a picture of the beast of burden. Remaining steady under control. It is an ox, not a racehorse, but yoked to a plow that pushes on steadily, persistently, no matter what the obstacles. It takes years for a fruit tree to bear fruit. That is why you don't give an important job that requires patience to a new Christian. They haven't yet developed patience. It doesn't come instantly. It takes time. The issue is are we going to let God be in control of our life, of our circumstances, of our children, of our spouse, or someone else? When we live in an uncertain world we can relax and say, "Yes, that wasn't the way I planned it but I don't have to get bent out of shape because God is in control." Patience shows that we have trusted God enough to let God be God!

b. Because God rewards patience. Worthwhile things take time to develop. James 5:17 says, "Be patient brethren, the farmer waits patiently for the precious fruit of the earth. You also be patient." Quality takes time to be developed. Nobody has more patience than the farmer does, who plants the seed and waits for the crop to become fruit. He waits patiently because he knows that that which is coming is worth the waiting. Meanwhile, that farmer doesn't stop working. He prepares the field, plants, and pulls weeds but ultimately all he can do is wait patiently for the good seed to mature. The biggest mistakes I have made in life where made when I have run ahead of God.

c. Because God is working things out. Often, behind the scenes in ways that we cannot even see, in ways that we have no clue,

The Good News About Hard Times

God is at work. In James 5:11, it reads, "You have heard of Job's perseverance and have seen what the Lord finally brought about. The Lord is full of compassion and mercy." What this is saying is that all the time that Job thought that God was doing nothing, God was actually working. All the time that Job was scratching his head, not knowing what was happening, God was working—all that time behind the scenes, out of sight. When the farmer plants the seed he has to wait for that seed to germinate, to sprout, and to grow. It is underground and we don't see anything. Nevertheless, it is happening. God is creating just the right conditions so that at just the right time, in the right way, there will be a harvest. The farmer waits. We wait, God works! Philippians 2:13, "God is at work within you." Maybe you can't see it, but He is. Romans 8:28, "And we know that in all things, God is working." In every circumstance in your life, God is working. Be patient! Let Him work! I don't know what kind of problem you have this week, but regardless of the problem you are going through—financial, relational, health—God is working on that problem. Be patient and trust Him. Remember this point: God's delays are not God's denials. That is a phrase worth writing down. Here's another:

"He may be slow, but he's never late". If you've been praying for an answer to a prayer and you haven't gotten it, the tendency is to think that God doesn't want to give it to us. No! Delay and denial are not the same thing. Sometimes God has to reach us in the same way that we want to teach our children. There is a difference between "No" and "Not yet." We want and we want it now, but we have to be patient. God is at work even when we don't see what is going on. Phillip Brooks, a famous pastor of the last century, was in his office one day, pacing back and forth, frustrated. Somebody walked in and said, "What is the matter, pastor?" He said, "I'm in a hurry and God isn't." God says, "Be patient because I am working things out behind the scenes."

So, when you feel that your hands may be tied and the situation may be uncontrollable, don't forget that God is working behind the scenes. Those who know say that bamboo will sometimes grow underground for a great distance and then suddenly grow through the ground and grow 12 feet in one day. Because God rewards patience, God will ultimately reward us. Verse 11, "From Job's experience we see how the Lord's plan finally ended in good." If we wait, patiently, God will reward us. One of my favorite Old Testament passages, that has meant a lot to me in times when I just did not know what God was doing, is in Joel 2:25. God says, "I will restore to you the years that the locust has eaten." What was Joel talking about? The locust years? In South Africa, there are still some years when the locusts swarm the land and eat the crops. They come in hoards, blocking out the sun. The crops are lost and a hard winter follows. The locusts years are feared and dreaded. However, in the year after the locust, South Africans harvest its greatest crops ever, for the dead bodies of locusts serve as fertilizer for the new seed and the locust year is restored as a bountiful crop swells the land. The Lord says, "I will restore to you the years that the locust have eaten." There are seasons of deep hurt and pain in all of our lives. Yet, the promise is that God will restore those "locust years" if we patiently endure. Fruitful times are waiting those who are patient in the hard times. Even as believers, there are times when we buy into the world's non-believing views. We act sometimes as if this life and this world are all we have. However, believers who merely trust the Lord are a different breed. We don't judge things simply by three score and ten years. God has all eternity to prove His faithfulness to us. The children of Israel waited more than a generation to go into the Promised Land. Many died off before the promise was kept. Sometimes the reward doesn't come in our lifetime. Many times in the Old Testament, the Bible says, "They walked with God." Our problem is that we sometimes run ahead of God and when we get ahead of God we often get into trouble. Patience protects us against premature action. We need to slow down and walk with Him at His pace. For many people, impatience is a constant irritant that takes much of the joy out of life.

III. What do I do in the waiting room?

We first have to look at life in light of eternity. We need to look at life through the glasses of eternity. Three times in three verses, 7, 8, and 9, it says the Lord is coming back someday. He is going to come back, just as certainly as He came 2000 years ago. We need to do what we are doing in light of His return.

a. Wait expectantly. We must expect a harvest. I must believe the harvest will happen probably not on our timetable, but that it is inevitable and that our patience is the right thing. What does a farmer do while he's waiting on God? Just sit in a lazy boy and watch reruns on TV all day long? Not at all! Having lived on a farm as a

The Good News About Hard Times

kid, I observed that the farmer was just as busy off harvest as during the harvest. What is he doing? He's preparing for the answer. He's getting ready. Waiting is a time for preparation for the harvest. That is when a farmer sharpens his equipment to be used for the harvest and does many, many other things.

I have pastored churches for over 39 years. In those 39 years, there was one point when I was not working in one specific church. I only had a part-time job, so I had time on my hands. I sat down and made a list of all the things I could do with my time that would help improve my skills and abilities as a preacher and pastor, to be ready for the harvest. I took intensive courses, one in preaching, another a communication class with one of the finest communications experts in America, Burt Decker out of San Francisco. I interviewed as a TV anchorman. I spoke almost every week in churches of several denominations, preaching or teaching classes. Since I had my doctorate in church growth, I began traveling and speaking for a Presbyterian evangelistic and renewal organization. I wrote and published some articles on church growth and did seminars on preaching. I traveled and spoke for them sometimes going back in the Midwest. Typically, I would go with a team of people, mostly lay people. We would go into declining churches, observe them for a few days, meet with Sessions and make some suggestions as to what to do to get their churches growing again. I had never typed nor used a computer. I'd always had secretaries, so I learned to do word processing on the computer. When I wasn't doing one of those things, I totally reorganized my sermon and teaching files and retrieval system. The point is that waiting time is preparation time! We demonstrate our trust in the Lord and our expectation in His faithfulness. How? By our preparation! We get ready for the answer in advance. Psalms 130:5, "...I wait expectantly, trusting God to help, for he has promised." What are you waiting for from God? Do you expect him to do something? Then, prove it! How can you prove you're expecting God to do something? Simple! What are you doing to get ready for it? Are you preparing for the answer? If the answer came today, would you be ready? The way you get ready for something is by preparing in advance. While you're waiting, you're preparing. Preparing demonstrates expectation. A lot of times when I am waiting on God, He's really waiting on me. He was willing to give me an answer a long time ago, but I wasn't ready to receive it. He's saying, "Grow up! Get some spiritual depth in your life...I want to bless your life, but you can't handle the blessing I want to pour on you. The blessing I want to pour on you is tremendous, but you are not ready to handle it." He is saying to us, "When you get some spiritual muscle in your life, I'll bless you beyond what you can imagine." Jesus waited 30 years before he began his ministry. Thirty years of preparation and He accomplished more in three years than we would in a lifetime. Isaiah 49:23, "The Lord says...no one who waits for my help will be disappointed."

b. Wait quietly. James points out that our impatience causes us to run off at the mouth and say just anything when we're irritated, when we're under pressure, when things aren't going our way, and when things aren't under our control. James warns of things to avoid. James 5:8-9, "Be patient. Do not grumble brethren one against the other that you may not be judged." He talks about grumbling right in the middle of patience because it is hard to keep quiet when you're frustrated. When you are frustrated you want everyone to know about it. You want to mumble, grumble, moan, and complain about it. James says, "Don't grumble." The New English Bible says, "Don't blame your troubles on one another." Do you hit the ground in the mornings griping? Is everything bad? When you get up in the morning, do you rise and whine? The high school kids that hang out at our house respond to one another when someone is complaining about something with, "Do you want some cheese with that whine?" James says in Verse 7, "Don't grumble about each other...or God will judge you. Behold the judge is standing at the door." James is warning us. So many times we make snap judgment about people simply based on external acts and so often those judgments turn out to be wrong. We all make inadequate judges. It is tremendously freeing not to have to judge people's hearts. Only the Lord can do that. Verse 9 says, "Don't blame your troubles on one another." James is saying that we are not to play the "blame game." Casting blame on everyone but ourselves (You made me do it!) we tend to blame others for our faults. The Lord says to us, "Grow up. Take responsibility for your own thoughts and actions." Don't point the finger at someone else. Patience, you will remember, is the fruit of the presence of the Holy Spirit in your life, not someone else's. Verse 12, "Above all else my friends, do not swear." Does waiting ever tempt you to swear? What happens when you get uptight? When you are frustrated and things aren't going your way, when things are beyond your control, how do you respond? Typically, we take it out on those closest to us. We unload on our husbands, our wives, or our children. We displace our anger on those that we love the most. James says, "Don't do that!"

c. Wait confidentially. James uses Job as an example. He says think about how others have endured suffering. Verse 10, "For examples of patience in suffering look at the prophets who spoke in the name of the Lord. Observe other people who are patient. We give great honor to those who endure under suffering. Job is an example of a man who endured, patiently." James was pointing out that patience is as contagious as is anger. He is saying that we learn patience just as we learn anger, so take into consideration those with whom you hang out. The way you respond in crises is not in your genes; it is in what you see in other people of influence in your life. You use as an excuse for losing your temper that you are a red head, or you are Italian, or your ancestors are from here, or there, or somewhere else and therefore you are not to blame. There is a big theological word for that—baloney! You learn how to handle anger from watching other people; you also learn patience from watching other people. That is why Proverbs 22:24, "Do not make friends with a hot-tempered person. Do not associate with one easily angered or you may learn his way and get yourself ensnared." You can learn to be patient. Verse 11, "You have heard of Job's perseverance." Paul wants us to persevere to the end, also. Keep on keeping on. Why? Verse 11 continues, "Job is an example of a man who endured patiently from his experience we have seen how the Lord's plan finally ended in good, for he is full of tenderness and mercy." How do you wait confidently? Sit still. Don't get nervous, anxious. You don't take matters into you own hands and work things out. You trust God and let Him work them out. Psalm 37:7, "Be still before the Lord and wait patiently for him to act." God's got it all planned out, everything is on schedule, nothing is late, and it is all moving toward a climax. God is in control.

My friends, here is the bottom line. We do not know what is going to happen tomorrow, much less next year or ten years from now. We don't know what the future holds, but we do know who holds the future. The point is that when Christ is in my life I don't have to control it. We don't have to feel as if we are holding it all together. We can relax because He's got it all under control. He knows what is best for us.

Jonathan H. Wilson

Have you ever gone from a bright room into a dark, dingy lighted room? You can do one of two things, you can immediately march right in, groping, and stumbling in the dark, knocking over furniture, risking injury, creating chaos; or, you can patiently wait until the eyes adjust to a new surrounding and then proceed safely. Sometimes when we are in the difficult space, we simply need to stop striving in the dark and simply wait on God and He will reward us. Patience is the ability to live in an uncertain world and relax; knowing that God is in charge. We can relax, not in blind ignorance, but because we know that God is at work moving toward His purpose. Patience is trusting that God knows what He is doing even though we can't understand all the details.

Where do you need to have patience? Do you have a situation in your life that seems outside your control? Maybe you're in a job situation and you are facing something beyond your control. Maybe you have had a financial reversal that was beyond your control. Maybe you have a long-term illness, or are taking care of someone who does. Maybe you've got an unchangeable person in your life and you are totally frustrated. It is frustrating when you tell your kids over and over again to do something and they don't do it. It is frustrating when you want to make a marriage work, and you are willing to change but your partner is not. It is frustrating when you have parents who are growing old, and they are stubborn and set in their ways and dependent upon you. Maybe you have a cantankerous person in your life and all they seem to do is upset you. They're never going to change. You need patience with an unchangeable person. You need patience with unexplainable problems.

Many of you would find a new joy if you could only hear the Lord saying, "Relax, you don't have to be in control of life. I will be in control. Trust me that I will do what is best for you and those you love." You see, that does take a lot of pressure off so we can be free to love, to be kind, and not to make giant issues of things that are not of eternal consequence; to see things in light of eternity.

There is great power in learning patience. Remember what God has said in James. God is in control. It may be out of your control, but it's not out of God's control. Nothing is beyond His power. His purpose for my life is greater than the problems I'm experiencing right now.

The Good News About Hard Times

My friends, God will reward our patience if not in this life, He will in eternity. God is working behind the scenes for a purpose. The Lord says, "I will restore to you the years that the locust have eaten." Be still in the presence of the Lord, and wait patiently for Him to act.

"Let go and let God be God!"

{James' nickname was "Old Camel knees because he had such big knots on his knees from spending hours and hours in prayer"

James 5:14 "Is any of you sick? He should call the elders of the church to pray over him, and anoint him with oil in the name of the Lord"}

"Old Camel Knees"

"The Mystery of prayer"

Book of James - Chapter 15

James 5:12-20

I heard of a parrot who, when bought by a pet lover, would constantly amuse people because it would say only one thing, "Let's neck!" A minister friend had a parrot, also, and one time when the minister was going on a vacation the pet lover offered to keep the minister's parrot. The minister's parrot also said only one sentence, "Let's pray!" So, as the minister was leaving town, he dropped by to leave the parrot for a few days. The first parrot said her usual "Let's neck!" to which the pastor's parrot, instead of its usual "Let's pray," said, "My prayers have been answered!" Oh, the secret of answered prayer.

A Newsweek cover story of a few years ago, reads, "The Mystery of Prayer." The article says that an overwhelming majority of Americans believe in prayer and believe that God answers prayer. In this article, the survey says that 54% of Americans say they pray every day; 29% say they pray several times a day. But, what do they understand about prayer?

The film "National Lampoons Christmas Vacation" illustrates the attitude many Americans have of prayer. With all the family gathered around the table, grandma recited the "Pledge of Allegiance" when she was asked to give the blessing.

This is the last in a series of 15 studies on the Book of James. I hope that you have gotten as much out of the Series as I have received. As James concludes his letter, the subject is "prayer." The word "prayer" is mentioned seven times in this passage. Prayer is what it is about. James had a reputation for being a man of prayer. His nickname was James, "Old Camel Knees," because he had such big knots on his knees from spending hours and hours in prayer. James is saying that there is tremendous power in prayer. Prayer is the greatest power in the Christian life and also the greatest privilege of the Christian life. Jesus said, "The things that I do, you'll do also even greater works."

Jonathan H. Wilson

How do you do greater works than Jesus? Jesus said, "It's by prayer." Let's look at some basic questions answered in this passage.

I. When should I pray?

1. When I am down emotionally. "Is any one of you in trouble? He should pray." (Verse 13a) The word in Greek literally means, "to suffer misfortune, to be in distress, to be under stress, under tension." In Timothy, it is translated "hardships," problems. He is talking about internal distress caused by external circumstances. James is talking about this in light of Verse 12 where James says, "Above all, my brothers, do not swear." When you are under tension, that is when you're tempted to swear. When you have distress in your life you have two alternatives—swear or prayer. (Verses 12 & 13)

A fly was looking up at a praying mantis, What are you doing?" said the fly. "I'm praying," said the mantis. "Don't be stupid, insects don't pray," the fly told it. And, at that the mantis swooped down and grabbed the fly in its claws and straight away the fly began, "Our Father, who art in heaven…" Like the fly, we should pray when under stress. Stress may be a financial crisis, a relational crisis, something on the outside, your heart is breaking, and tension is at an all-time high. David said in Psalm 18:4, "In my distress I call unto the Lord." Our Lord wants us to pray about our problems, any problems that are causing stress in our life. However, when we are in trouble is not the only time we should pray. We should also pray when:

2. When emotionally upset. James says, "Is anyone happy? Let him sing songs of praise." (Verse 13b) Have you noticed that life is a series of alternations between high and low, feast to famine, problem to joy? The Bible says, "Weep with those who weep and rejoice with those who rejoice." One of the job qualifications of being a pastor is that you have to be willing to shift gears pretty quickly. You can be counseling a couple to be married one minute and planning a memorial service the next. A lot of people are up and a lot of people are down. Sometimes it is difficult to go from one directly to another. However, in everyone's life there are situations when you're down, and when you're down you pray. When you're happy, live it to the hilt. Some people are afraid that if they really enjoy what God is doing then He's going to zap them with a bummer. They think, "If I think it's great, then the bottom is bound to fall out. It's too good!" They're afraid to pray. They're afraid to rejoice. It is not uncommon

The Good News About Hard Times

for someone new to come to our church. Recently, a first-time visitor said, "The upbeat spirit here is contagious. You can really sense it." I think Christians ought to be contagious. I think it ought to be fun to go to church. The Bible says, "I was glad when they said unto me, let us go into the house of the Lord," not sad, mad, or bummed out—glad! So, when you're happy, you sing. On Sunday morning it is a celebration—a day of joy. James says it's valid to be happy. You say you don't like to sing praise music? "Praise" is used 550 times in the Bible. It is to be the lifestyle of the Christian—to be happy. If you want the secret of a rich, personal, upbeat life, nothing has done more for my own personal life than two things (1) having a sense of humor, and (2) singing to the Lord. I sing a lot when I am alone in the car, whereas anywhere else I would be too inhibited. Some years ago I went I went back to my Dad's funeral. I drove across Tennessee, by myself, in a state of doom and gloom. I stopped and bought Christian tapes and put them on to soothe the grief, and I sang songs the rest of the way across the State. By the time I had arrived, I was in good shape to preach at my Dad's funeral and to minister to the family with a true sense of joy. I hope that you have several Christian tapes. Patty goes to sleep every night listening to Christian CD's. She has worn out many tape recorders and CD players over the years. I listen when I study and when I'm in the car. Someone has said, "Pray when you feel like it, pray when you don't feel like it, and pray until you do feel like it."

3. When I am hurting physically. James 5:14-15, "Is any one of you sick? He should call the elders of the church to pray over him, and anoint him with oil in the name of the Lord. And the prayer offered in faith will make the sick person well; the Lord will raise him up. If he has sinned, he will be forgiven." The word "sick" that is used here literally means "without strength." You are totally wasted, fatigued, bedridden, and unable to work. This is not just acid indigestion or postnasal drip. This is a serious illness here that is keeping him from actually working. It's the word most frequently used for illness. It is the same word describing Lazarus. When Lazarus got sick, he died. And, the same word describes the man at the pool of Bethesda who sat there for years and years and didn't have enough energy to get up and get into the pool. James is talking about a serious illness here. The elders of the church are to come and pray over the person and anoint him with oil. This is where the anointing ritual in the Catholic Church originated. The person is so sick that they are

close to death and the priest comes in and anoints the person with oil. Gradually over the years, this has become known as the "unction for the dead," better known as "last rites." Does God heal today? I believe that He does. In fact, I believe He never stopped healing. The Scripture teaches that there are three different kinds of sickness.

A. Three Kinds of Sickness

1. Sickness for our homecoming. The Bible says that first there is the sickness for death. It's covered in 1 John 5:16, and John 11:4. In that kind of sickness God allows to take us on home to be with Him. Reality tells us that we are all terminal. None of us leave this earth alive. There are some sicknesses from which you never recover. If every sickness could be healed by faith then anybody who had a lot of faith would never die. There is a sickness for the purpose of taking you on home.

2. Sickness for discipline. The purpose for a sickness for discipline is covered in 1 Corinthians 11:28-32 where they were abusing the Lord's Supper. Paul said that because they were abusing the Lord's Supper, some of them were sick. The Lord is disciplining them because they're out of the will of God. When we sin it can bring sickness into our lives.

3. Sickness for the glory of God. The sickness for the glory of God is a sickness that God has allowed in your life simply because He wants to heal you of it and let it be a testimony to the world. John 11:4, a man came to Jesus who was ill and blind. The Disciples said, "Lord, who's sinned, him or his parents?" Jesus said, "Nobody's sinned, this is a sickness for the glory of God." Then, he healed the guy and it brought glory to God. The last is the kind of sickness that God wants to heal.

B. Five Attitudes Toward Healing

1. Sensationalists. These are the guys you see on television. They come into town and hold giant meetings in large auditoriums, and advertise miracles. There are bright lights and TV cameras rolling. Often, the healer is flamboyant. He shouts at the people and slaps them on the head. It is often a highly charged emotional atmosphere. Be careful of this. Be discerning. I don't see Jesus doing this. He did the exact opposite in His healing. In all of Jesus' healing He took

The Good News About Hard Times

them aside from the crowd where they are out of the glare of the public, talked with them on a one-on-one basis, healed them there, and then it was reported to the crowd. Jesus never manipulated people and never used them for show. He always cared about their needs more than He did about making an impression on the crowds. He healed people quietly.

2. Name it, claim it. These people say that it is always God's will for everybody to be healed. This is the "Name it and Claim it" group. Sickness is a result of sin and all you need to do is claim your healing and God will heal. I claim I have a Cadillac and I get a Cadillac! The problem with this is that it makes God a genie. All of a sudden God is serving me, my needs, my whims, rather than my serving Him. If you're not healed you lack faith. The result is that if there is no healing there is tremendous guilt. "Maybe I just didn't believe enough." False doctrine always creates false guilt. Always! That's one of the problems with legalism. When you make up all of these rules and regulations, it takes the joy of knowing Jesus out of your life. The Bible says, "Where the Spirit of the Lord is, there is liberty."

3. Not since Bible Times. These people say the gifts of healing were only for New Testament times and they're no longer around. They believe the age of miracles is past. "Yes, God did heal at one time in human history, but that day is over. Don't bother looking for those gifts." Let's look at church history for a moment. The first three centuries of the church are noted for their continuing healing ministries. Gradually, the number of healing occurrences diminished. By the time of St. Augustine there were very few. This brilliant theologian explained that certain miraculous events were needed only in the first century. And, since the canon was completed there is no need for God to work in that way. What Augustine did, primarily, was to adjust his theology to his experience. The fact that he was not experiencing healings convinced him that they were not meant to be. I understand that in the last three years of his ministry he observed an outbreak of miraculous healings. However, this was too late to go into his major writing accomplished much earlier in his career. I find it interesting to observe that the Bible, at no point, denies the ongoing possibility for healing. Not only that but Hebrews 13:8 says, "Jesus Christ is the same yesterday, today, and forever."

4. Rationalists. These are the people who say that it is just all in your mind. If you are ill, it's because you think you're ill. Just deny it and

you will be okay. This includes the Christian Science, among others. Just deny it is happening and it will go away.

5. Realists. I think our Life-Coach James would be a realist. This recognizes two facts. One, the fact that God still does heal. He does heal but not everybody gets healed. That is also a fact of life. God does heal people today. Two, He doesn't heal everybody. I think life is an example of that. The true gift of healing is pretty rare; even in the Book of Acts miraculous healings were rare. Only three people are described as using the gift of healing—Peter, in Acts 9:33; Philip, in Acts 8:6; and Paul, in Acts 28:8. Notice when Paul described his "affliction" which was most likely an eyesight problem, to the Corinthians in 2 Corinthians 12:7-9, Paul does not claim healing for himself but he has learned that God had given him sufficient grace. Likewise, when he writes Timothy (1 Timothy 5:23) who at the time suffered a stomach ailment, Paul does not prescribe prayer for healing. He rather prescribes a little wine. When Epaphroditus was nearing death, Paul gave no indication of attempting to use his gift of healing. (Philippians 2:25) So, we know healing may or may not happen. But, it can happen! So, how do we go about doing it?

C. What to do?

1. Take the initiative. So what does James say to do when you are sick? You, "He should call the elders." Who is doing the calling? The sick person. Who does he call? Call the Elders of the church. James says you call the spiritual leaders of your church to pray for you. These guys aren't professional healers who go around holding healing meetings. This also implies support for belonging to a local church. Every Christian needs to identify himself with a particular body of believers. Why? One good reason is that when you get sick, you know whom to call. You have a church family to call for help and healing. In the New Testament, there was no such thing as a free-floating "church shopper" who would just float around, listen to Christian radio and TV, and bounce around from this church to that church. There were no such things in the New Testament. Every person was a member of a specific local church, because it says you are the body and each of you are members of it. The value of it is when you're sick or in need there is somebody there to care for you, such as Elders and Deacons. Our church is a praying church. When someone in our church is sick or has some kind of emergency need, our church prays during its worship services, through the prayer

The Good News About Hard Times

chain, through the Deacons, and through our special "homebound prayer warriors." The Deacons also often help church members in times of financial crises or hospitalization. Or, they set up memorial service receptions. That is one of the privileges of being a part of a local church instead of floating around from church to church and never really being a part of a church family. We won't, but Faith and I could, tell you some sad stories about how gloomy a memorial service was because the people never joined a church family and got involved. Nobody really knew them. It seems as if they were always looking for the perfect church, so they never joined one. You can tell the difference, immediately, when someone is sick in our church family and elders are called and notified. It makes a huge difference. Non-members are not excluded, but you all know people care about those they know about. And, if someone does not join a group, they will probably never really feel a part of the group. Those that are members find out that there are a lot of caring things that happen when people are members of a church and they notify the elders of their illness. By the way, deacons were elected in the Early Church, when the elders were overwhelmed with such needs allowing the elders to focus on leading and guiding the vision and the future of the church. The Deacons could then focus on the sick. The sick person takes the initiative to do what?

2. Call for the elders to pray. "...to pray over him...." The guy is probably in bed, so they are praying over him. He is seriously ill. "...and anoint him with oil." Now, there is some difference of opinion on the anointments with oil. Some see it as a sacred symbol of the Holy Spirit. Others see it as medicine. Oil was used both ways in Biblical times. Two words in the Greek that are translated "anoint" are (1) Chrio, from which we get the word Christ. This means to anoint sacredly like Elijah anointed the king with oil. (2) Alepho means to anoint the body in a physical way. It is the word that Jesus uses to describe what the Good Samaritan did to the wounded man. He anointed the wounded man with healing oil. James uses the second word in this verse. This word is never used in the New Testament with a sacred meaning. Doctors were very scarce in those days. Home remedies were always tried between the time the person was diagnosed ill and before a doctor could be found and come from a distance. Olive oil was the medicine of the day. It had such medical qualities that it was used for just about everything. It was like today's antibiotic perhaps used a painkiller, or penicillin, or an operation

for the relief of physical pain. The text indicates that two extremes should be avoided. One is to pray and to refuse medical help; and, the other is to use physicians but never pray. The advice of James includes both pills and prayer.

3. Get the best medical help. In New Testament times they did use oil to rub onto people, to massage, use as a salve. There was a medicinal value in that. Remember the Good Samaritan when he found the man at the side of the road? He took the man and applied oil and wine to his wounds and then bandaged him up. Oil was used for medicinal purposes. Call the Elders and ask them to pray. "...in the name of the Lord..." The point is this; God is the healer, not any person. The name represents the character of the Lord. All healing is based on God's character. And, finally...

4. When I am hurting spiritually. "Therefore confess your sins to each other and pray for each other so that you may be healed." (Verse 16a) In Jesus' day, and in many places today, it is taught that all sickness is a result of sin. They teach that if you are ill, then supposedly, you had some hidden sin in your life. If you confessed and still were sick then you still had some other hidden sin. Jesus blew that idea out of the water in John 9 where he said to the man who had been born blind that nobody sinned. I think that this is a very unfair concept. You think of babies being born with birth defects—obviously, that baby hasn't sinned. We live in a fallen world and part of the cause is that there are hurts and problems. On the other hand, Jesus did teach that some of the sickness in our lives we do bring upon ourselves. If I don't follow God's principles, my body is going to find out about it. If I don't take care of my body—eat right, sleep right, exercise right—then all kinds of ailments will come upon me. If I don't listen to God's word where it says, "Don't be anxious about anything, but pray about everything," and I worry, fret, get anxious, and get an ulcer, then I am to blame for it. It is amazing that some doctors actually prescribe prayer for their patients. Isn't it ironic that the medical world seems to believe in prayer more than in the church? Of family practitioners surveyed, 99% believed that a patient's spiritual beliefs contribute to healing. Eleven medical schools, including Harvard and Johns-Hopkins, offer courses in prayer and healing. Doctors say "It's not so much what you eat, but what's eating you that makes the difference." If I don't trust God, and if I allow these things to come into my life, there will be sin. "Therefore confess your sins to each other and

The Good News About Hard Times

pray for each other so that you may be healed." Why isn't everybody healed? I don't know. God has the power but it isn't His purpose in different situations. It is always in God's power to heal but it is not always in God's purpose to heal. A clear example of this is Paul, In 1 Corinthians. It said Paul prayed three times for God to heal a problem in his life but three times God said, "No, I've got a better plan for you." What is the condition for healing? Confess. We'd rather conceal and camouflage our sins than to confess them. It is a liberating experience to confess your sins and get them out and share them, not just with the Lord but with each other. Revealing your feeling is the beginning of healing. Many people come to me in counseling and begin by saying, 'I've never told this to anyone else in the world." Once they say that, I know that something great is going to happen. I know what a relief it is to not carry a burden anymore, to get it out and share it with somebody else so you can be loved and accepted for who you are without having to wear a mask and pretend that you are perfect. "...confess to each other." Does that mean I get up and confess to the whole church? I don't think so, though some churches still teach that. There is a principle of the Circle of Confession. Only confess as widely as it involves other people. If I've got a private sin, just between the Lord and me, then I ought to just confess it to the Lord. If it's a personal sin, between you and me, then I need to come to you. If it involves somebody else, you ought to go to somebody else. If it is a public sin, then I need to apologize to the whole church. He says confess your sins, not broadcast them. There ought to be at least one person—husband, wife, pastor, friend—you have that you can share everything with and know you'll be loved and accepted unconditionally. A verse in Job says, "A man needs his friend most when he's doubting God." He needs somebody to stand and walk him through that time of doubt to that time of faith. When Christians really love each other you have to lock the doors to keep people out. The Bible says, "By this shall all men know that you're my disciples, that you love each other." That's what counts. In New Testament times, the Christians confessed to each other. During the Dark Ages, they confessed to the priests. Protestants said, "We're not going to confess to anybody!" As a result, we've got a lot of problems and hang-ups. When should I pray? James says you can pray whenever you've got a need—a physical need, an emotional need, a material need. No matter what it is, you ought to pray.

Jonathan H. Wilson

II. What Kind of Person Can Pray?

"Elijah was a man just like us..." (Verse 17a) Who can pray? Some people think you have to be a spiritual giant to pray and get those kinds of answers. "I could never pray and see somebody healed," or "I could never pray and see a financial miracle." Many Christians feel inferior. James uses Elijah as an illustration. "Elijah was a man just like us..." When James speaks about Elijah you need to understand that he isn't talking about his power, but simply Elijah's calling for God's power and purpose. James says, "Look, Elijah was a man just like you." Notice the word "earnestly." When we pray earnestly it shows God that the answer really matters to us. Look at children or especially grandchildren. What is it like when you take them to the store and they see something they want? They ask for it earnestly, don't they? And then they ask for it again and again, and again. If they are creative, they'll think up a dozen different ways to remind you that they want candy, or a toy, or a certain food. Why do they do that? Because it's important to them that they get the things they ask for. So, they work at getting your attention. The lesson of Elijah's life is you don't have to be perfect to pray. You don't have to be perfect to see answers to your prayers. It's for ordinary people. 1 Kings 18, Elijah got alone with God and humbled himself praying for rain. It says he prayed seven times. He was persistent. He would not give up. One day a little cloud formed in the sky and Elijah got his umbrella and said, "It's going to be a gusher!" The rains came and flooded the place. God uses ordinary people like you and Elijah to do extraordinary things through prayer.

III. How Can I Pray Effectively?

That same Newsweek article says that 85% of Americans say they accept God's failure to grant their prayers, so how can we be more effective in our prayers? I want to review four conditions for praying effectively that James mentions in his book.

1. I must ask. "You do not have, because you do not ask God." (James 4:2) That sounds simple but in a lot of our prayers we never ask for anything. We say, "Thank you for..." and "Bless..." and that's it. We never pray specifically. The more specific your prayers are the greater you are going to be blessed in the answer. Elijah also prayed specifically in his prayers. He didn't just ask for God to bless Israel, he prayed for rain. He was asking for a specific answer in response

The Good News About Hard Times

to his prayer. When you pray, "God bless such and such..." how do you know if God answers the prayer? Throw away all your cliches. I love to hear new Christians pray because they don't know all the language and they're so honest. It is refreshing.

2. Have a right motive. "When you ask, you do not receive because you ask with the wrong motives that you may spend what you get on your pleasures." (James 4:3) You don't receive often times because of wrong motives, but when persistent with the right motives the chances for the answer you desire increases in likelihood. "He prayed earnestly that it wouldn't rain and it didn't rain on the land for three and a half years. He prayed again and the heavens gave rain and the earth produced its crops." (1 Kings 19) What was Elijah's motive? To overcome a drought that was starving good people.

3. A Clean life. "The prayer of a righteous man is powerful and effective." (James 5:16b3) Now, we're not talking about works and righteousness. We're not talking about perfection. We're talking about righteousness. Righteousness is our standing before God when you became a believer. It has nothing to do with your perfection. If God only answered the prayers of perfect people, how many prayers would get answered? None! But, on the other hand, God does want us to have a clean life. However, listen carefully—good works are a response to, not a prerequisite for, righteousness. When Norman Vincent Peale was a boy he found a big, black cigar; he slipped into an alley and lit it up. It didn't taste good but it made him feel grown up—that is, until he saw his father coming. Instantly, he put the cigar behind his back and tried to look very casual. Desperate to divert his father's attention, Norman pointed to a billboard advertising a coming circus. "Can I go to the circus daddy? Please, when it comes to town can we go?" His father's response taught Norman a lesson he never forgot. "Son", he answered firmly but quietly, "never make a petition while at the same time trying to hide smoldering disobedience."

Psalm 66:18, David said, "If I hide or [conceal] iniquity [sin] in my heart then the Lord will not hear." If I am willfully and knowingly doing something I know is displeasing to God and say, "God, I'm going to continue doing this but, by the way, help me out." It's like saying, "Dad, will you loan me the keys to the car, but I'm never going to do a single thing you ask." We need to have a clean life before Him. Proverbs 28:9, "He that turneth his back from the hearing of the law, even his prayers are an abomination." (Isaiah 59:2) Your sins have separated you between you. Your God has hid His face so He cannot hear." I remember counseling a person years ago who was concerned and even angry with God because their prayers had not been answered. At the same time, they were known in the church as a primary source of spreading gossip about people. Verse 16 says, "Therefore confess your sins to each other and pray for each other so that you may be healed." When the word, therefore, is found in the Bible you need to go back and see what the author was talking about. James is saying that when a person prays in faith, God answers and forgives when we confess our sins to one another. In other words, prayer has so much power and potential we don't want to jeopardize prayer's effectiveness. Maybe the reason why we aren't getting healed or it doesn't seem like God is getting through is because there is unconfessed sin toward one another. We might have asked God to forgive us, but we haven't asked the person. This is not like when we were kids and we would use a middleman to tell someone we forgave them. James is saying that if you have wronged someone you need to go to that person and seek his or her forgiveness. Confess your faults to one another and spend time praying for one another so that you might be healed. Look at what is at stake here! Your healing might be a prayer away. Your answer might be a prayer away, but sin is blocking that from happening. What is it that keeps us from becoming powerful people of prayer? The message reads, "The prayer of a person living right with God is something to be reckoned with."

4. Ask in faith. "But when he asks, he must believe and not doubt…" (James 1:6) Expect an answer when you come to God. Believe that He wants to answer your prayer. Trust Him. Don't doubt. Really believe. However, that obviously doesn't mean that God heals, as we would like. We have to trust that God knows what He is doing and will provide healing that fulfills His purpose.

One of my favorite Christian Preacher/Teachers is Tony Campolo. I go to hear him every chance I get. He tells the story about being in a church in Oregon where he was asked to pray for a man who had cancer. Campolo, as he always does prayed boldly for the man's healing. Soon Tony got a phone call from the man's wife. She said, "Tony, You prayed for my husband. He had cancer." She continued, "He died." Campolo, of course felt terrible. The wife continued, "But, Tony I don't want you to feel bad. When he came to the church that Sunday he was filled with anger. He knew that he was going to be

The Good News About Hard Times

dead in a short period of time and he hated God. He was only 58 years old and he wanted to see his children and grandchildren grow up. He was angry that this so called "All-powerful God" didn't take away his sickness and instantly heal him. He would lie in bed and curse God and everyone else. The more his anger grew towards God, the more miserable he was to everyone around him. It was becoming miserable to be in his presence." The lady told Campolo, "After you prayed for him a peace had come over him and a joy had come into him. Tony, the last few days have been the best of our lives. We've sung, we've laughed, we've read Scripture, we've prayed. Oh, they've been wonderful days and I called to thank you for laying your hands on him and praying for healing." Then, she said something incredibly profound. She said, "He wasn't cured, but... he was healed."

Printed in the United States
By Bookmasters